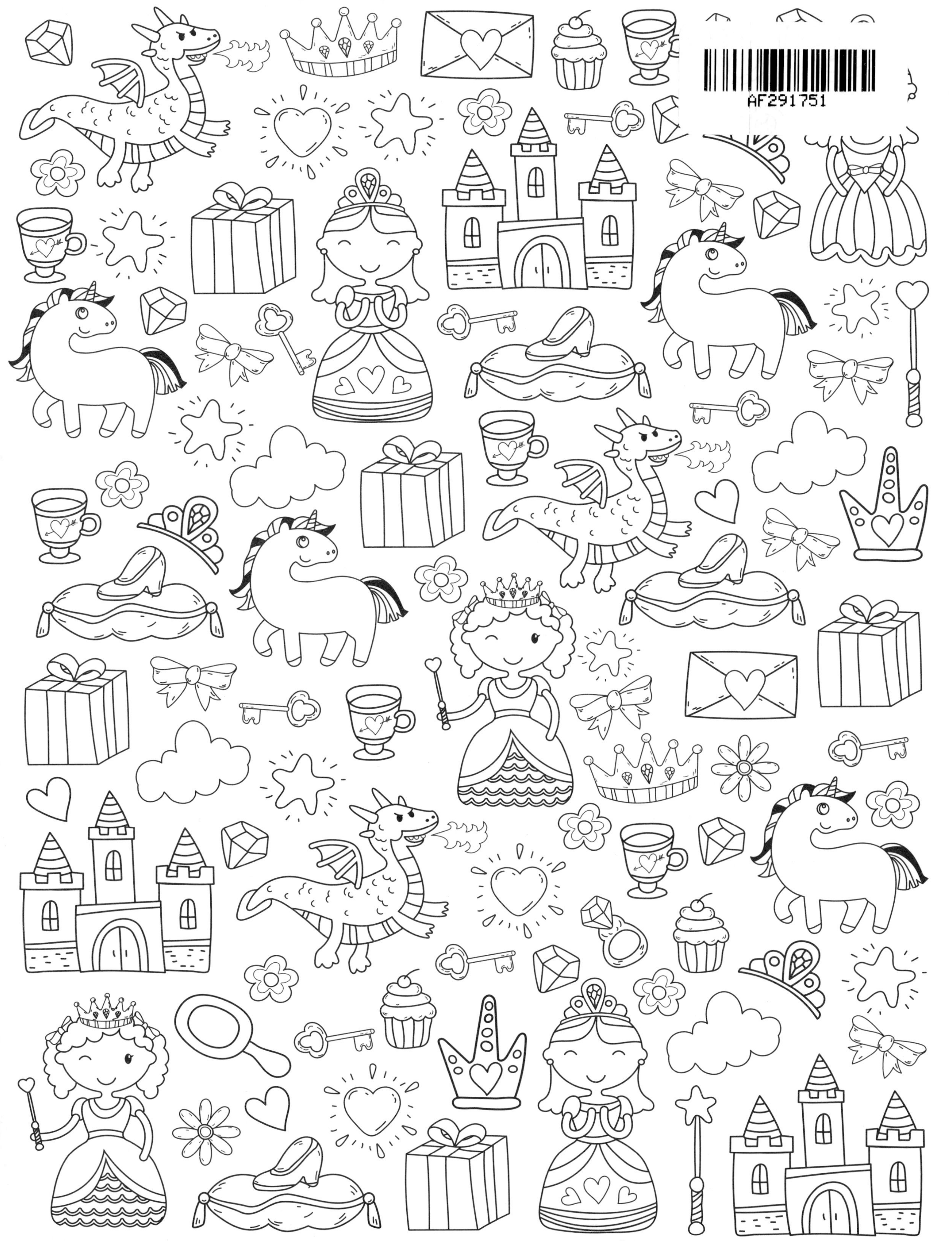
AF291751

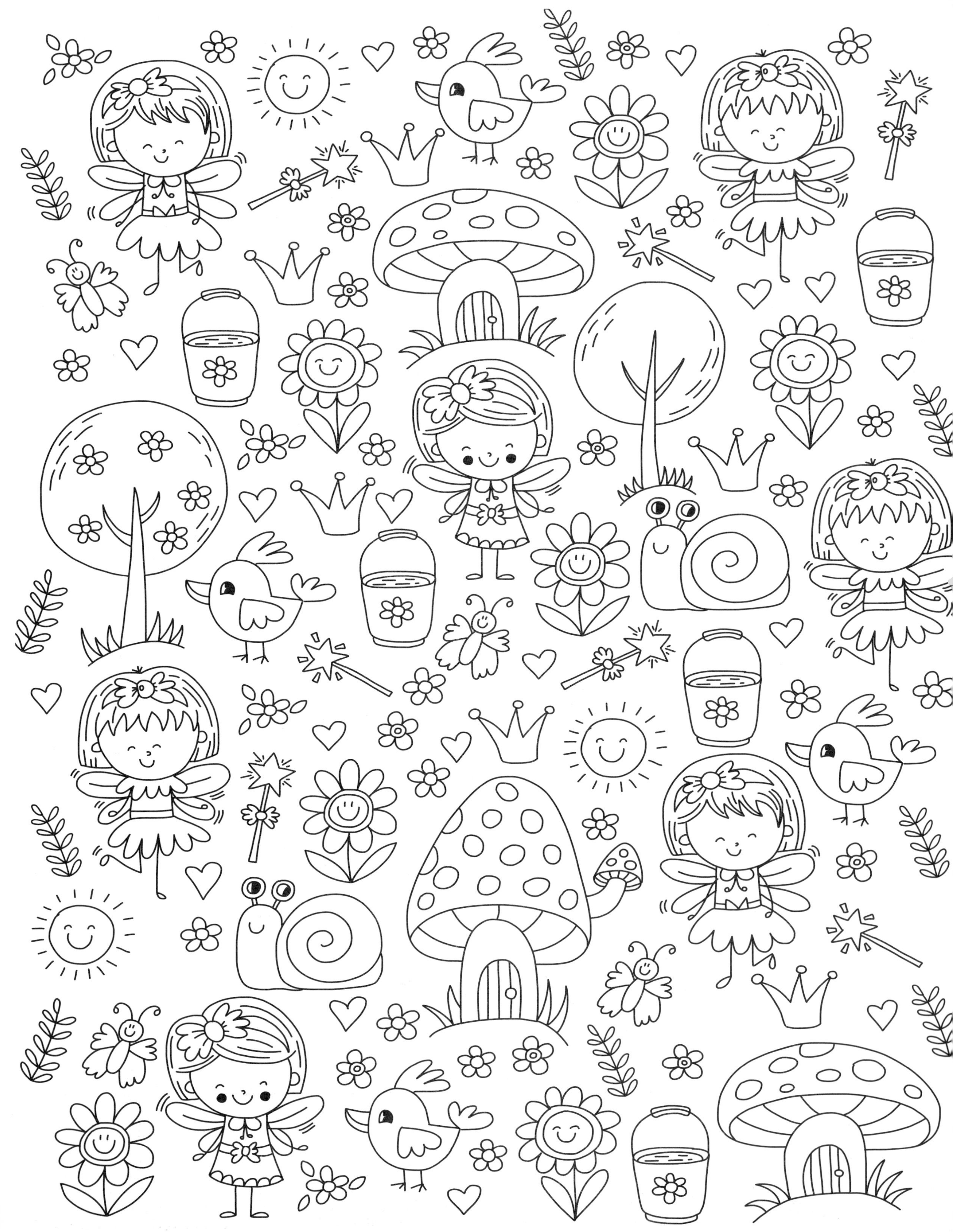

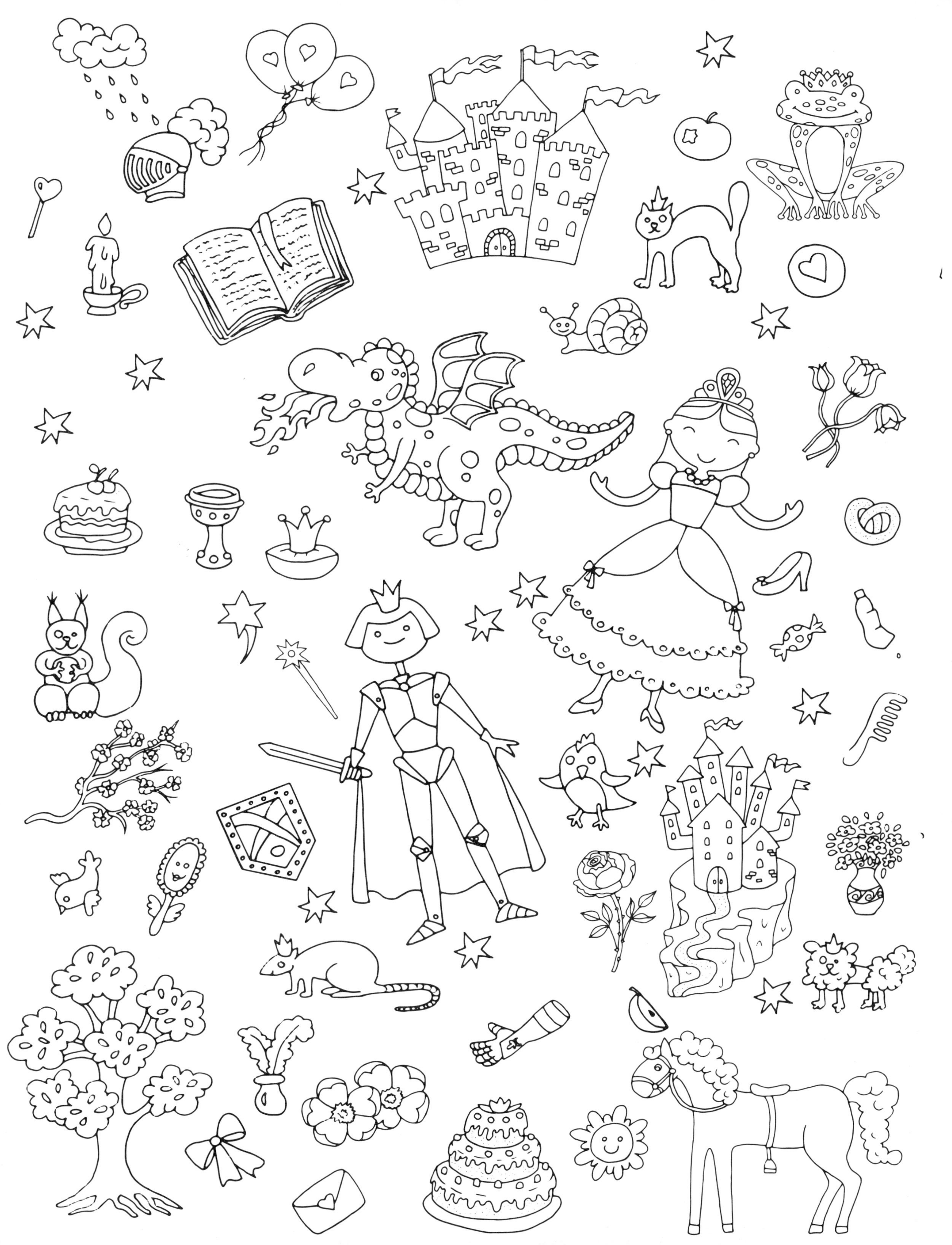

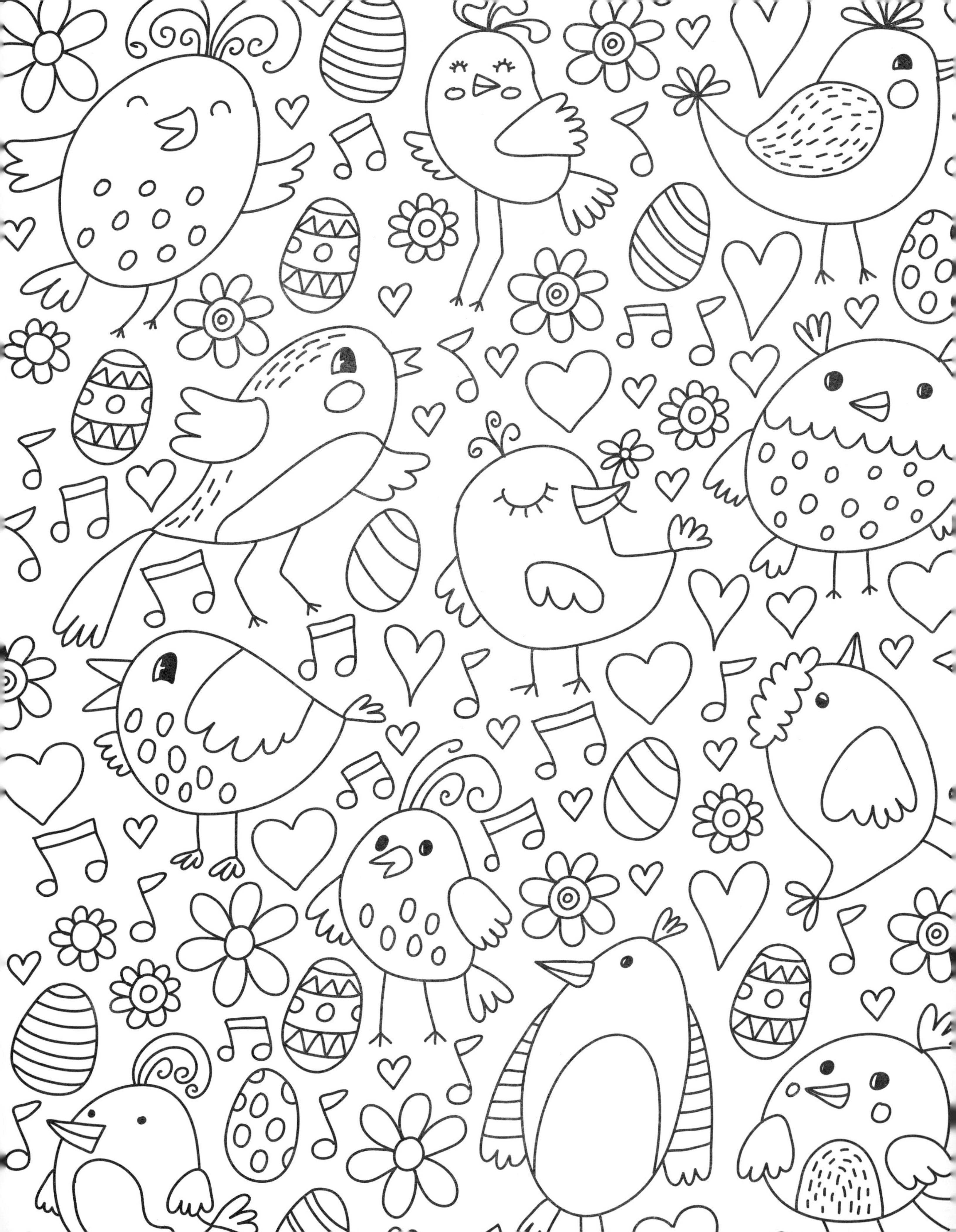

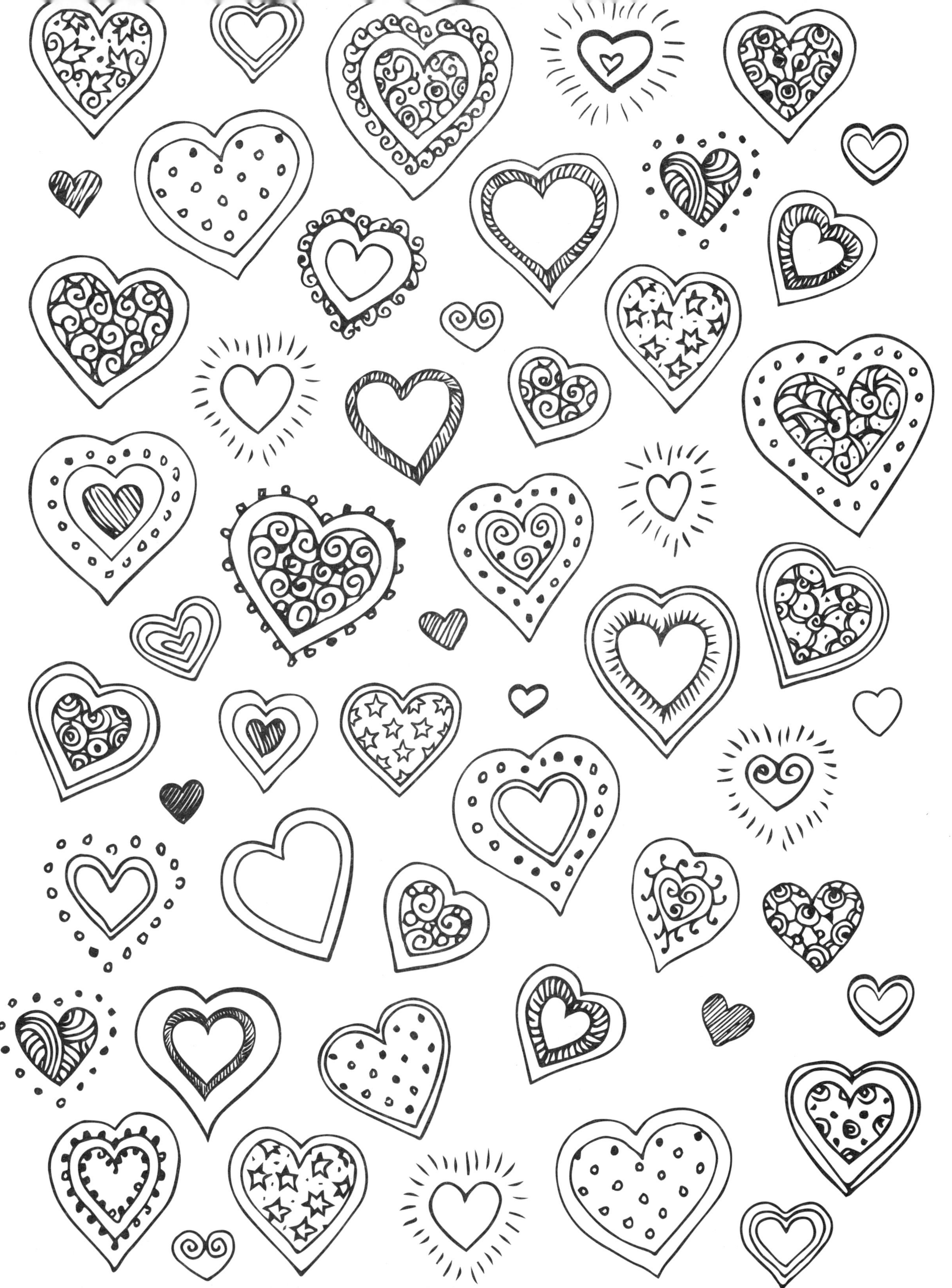

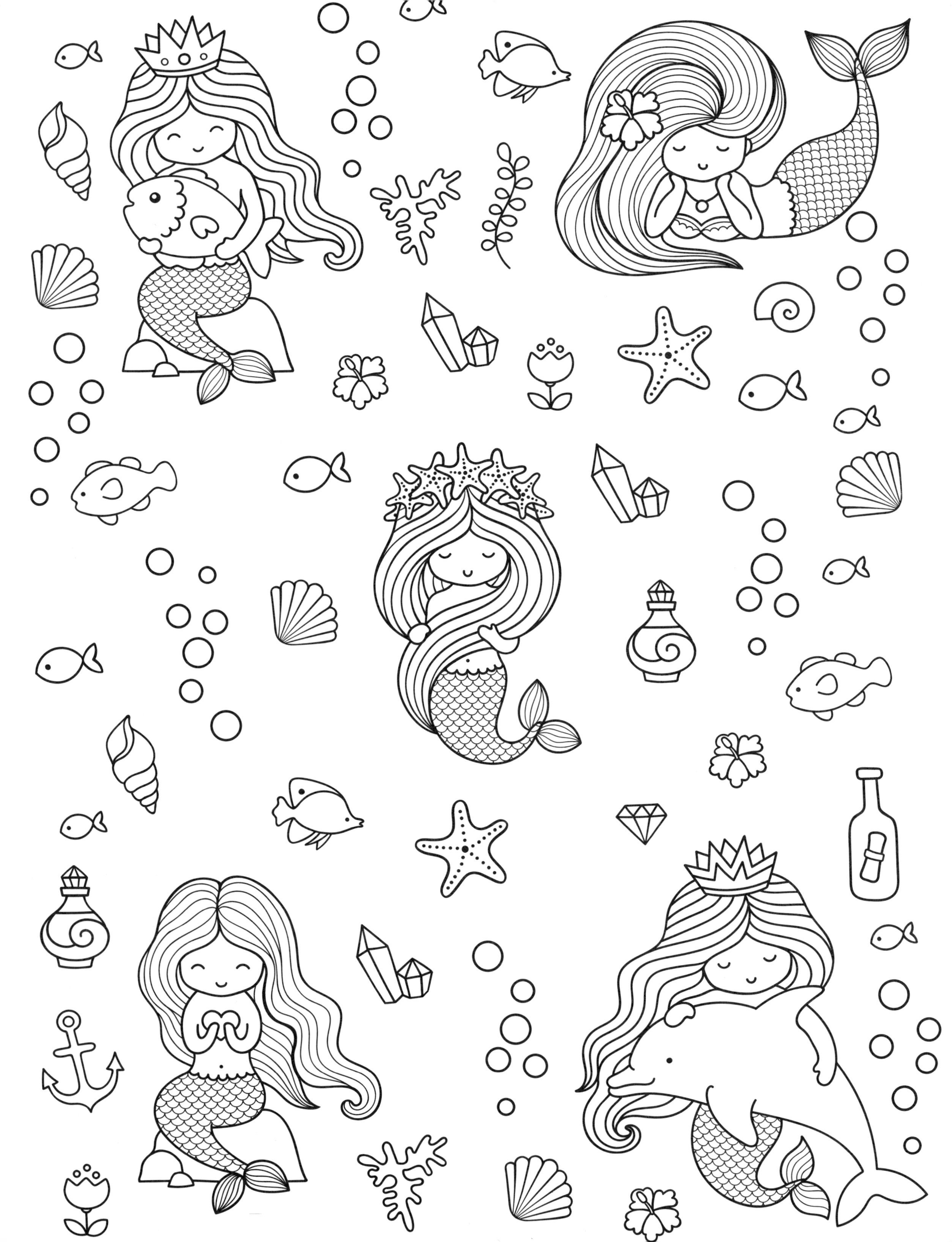

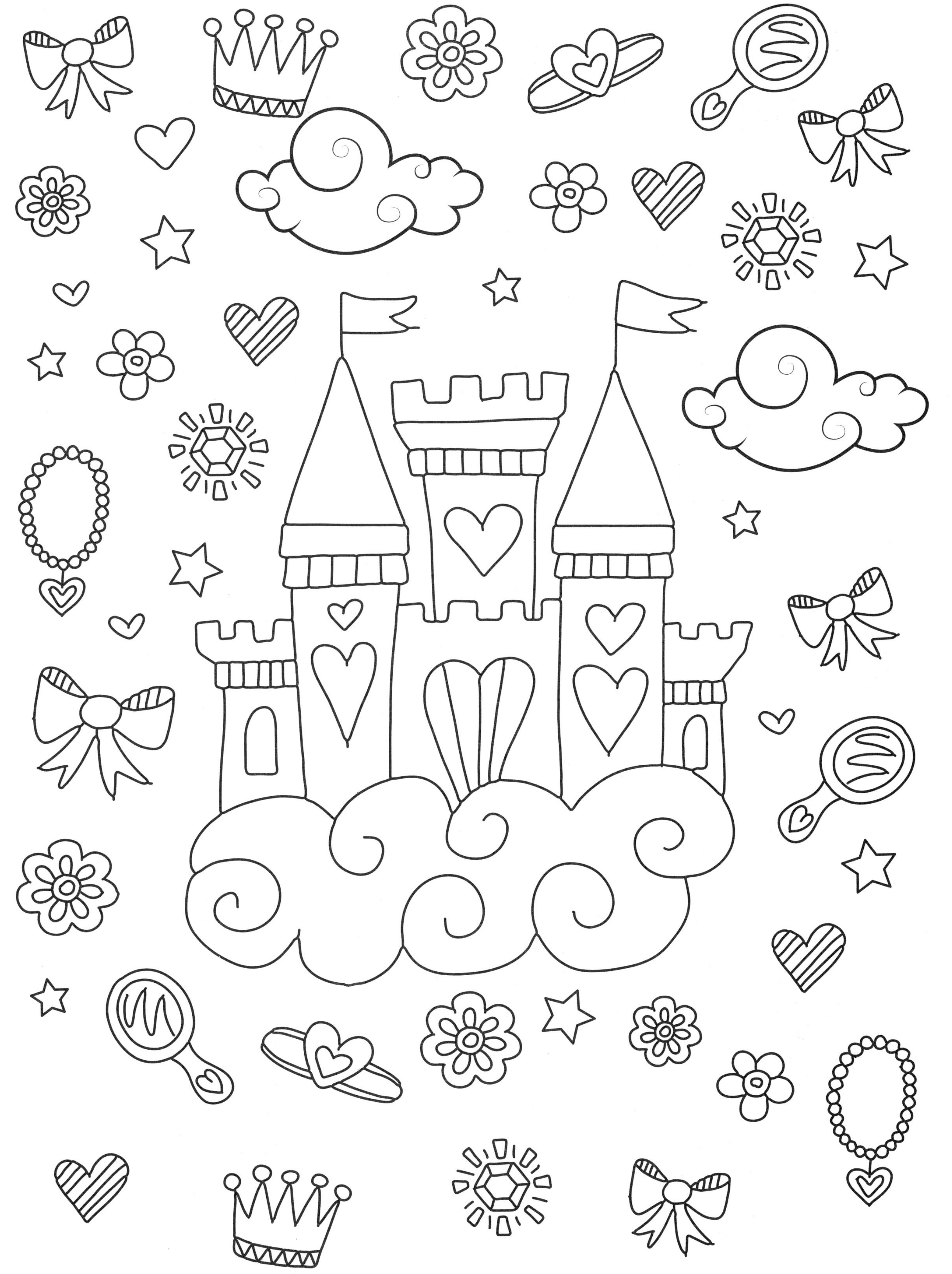

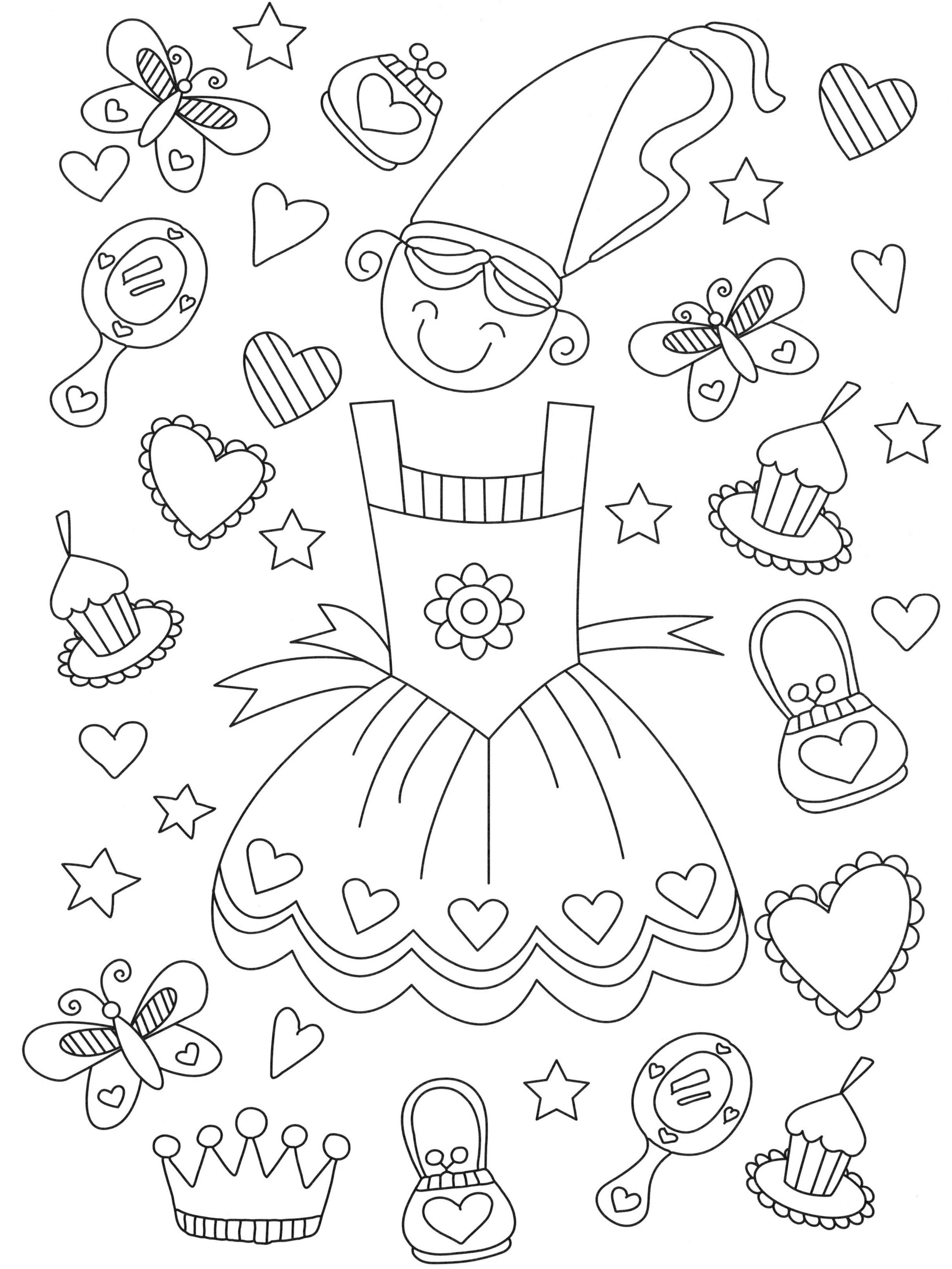

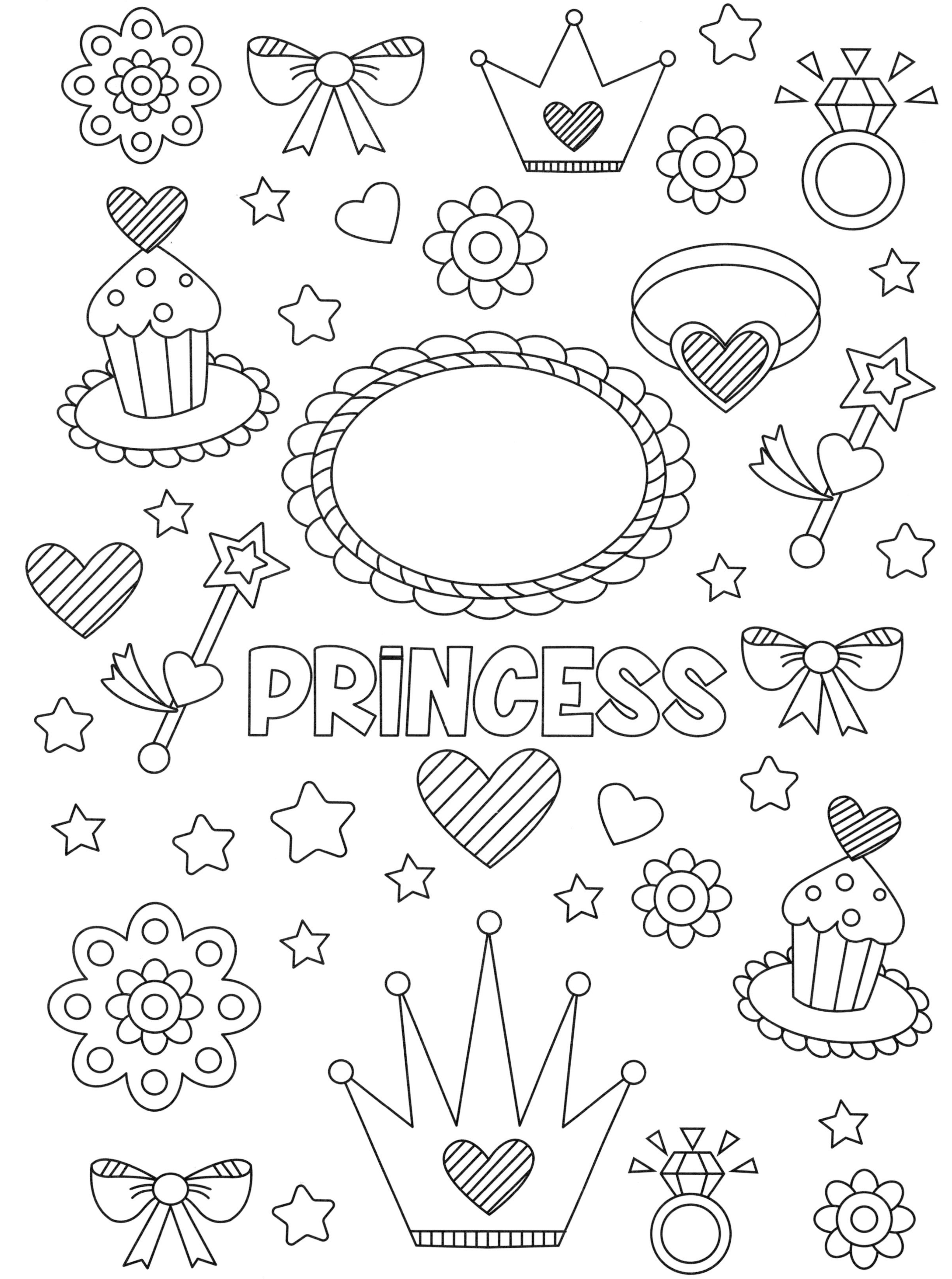
PRINCESS

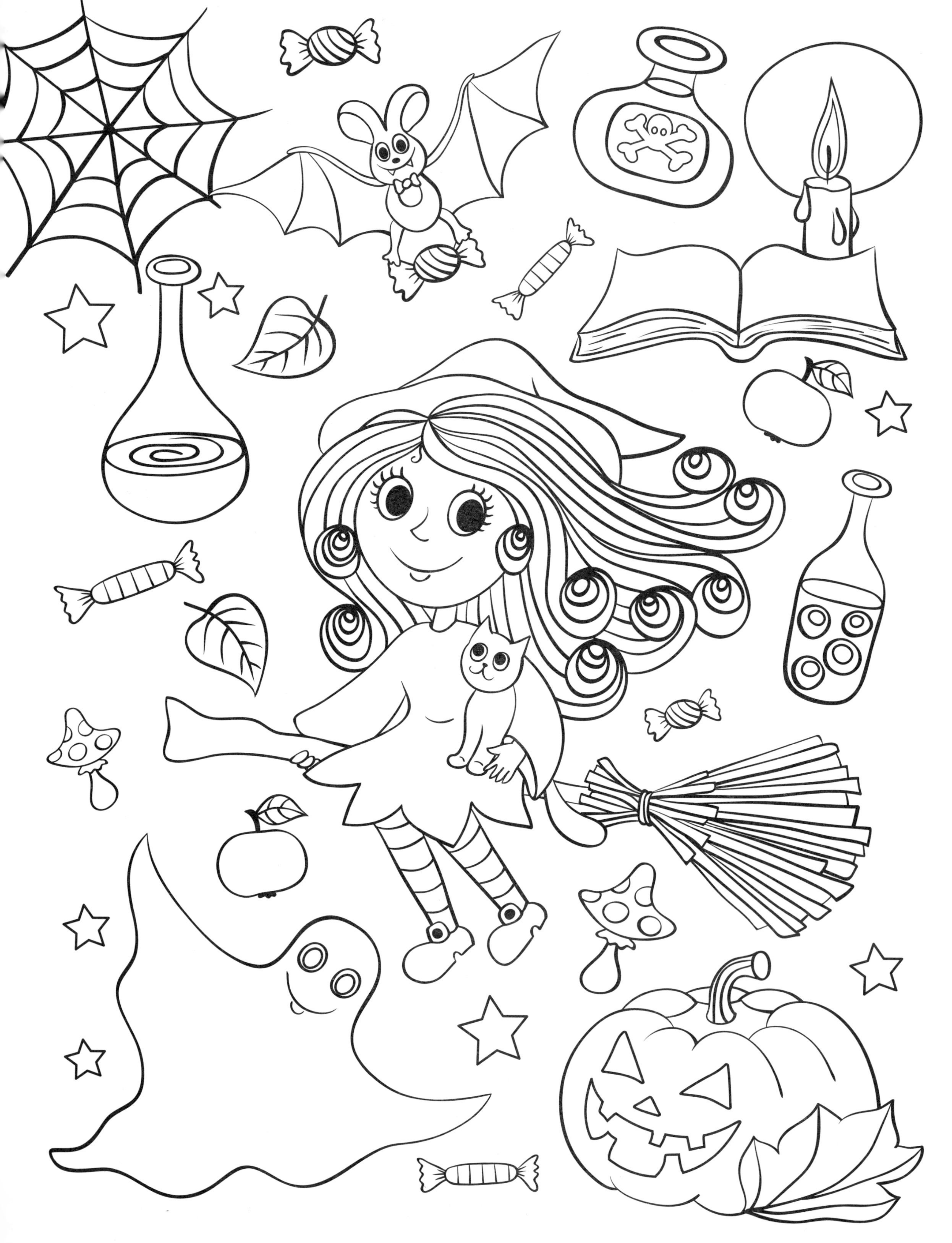

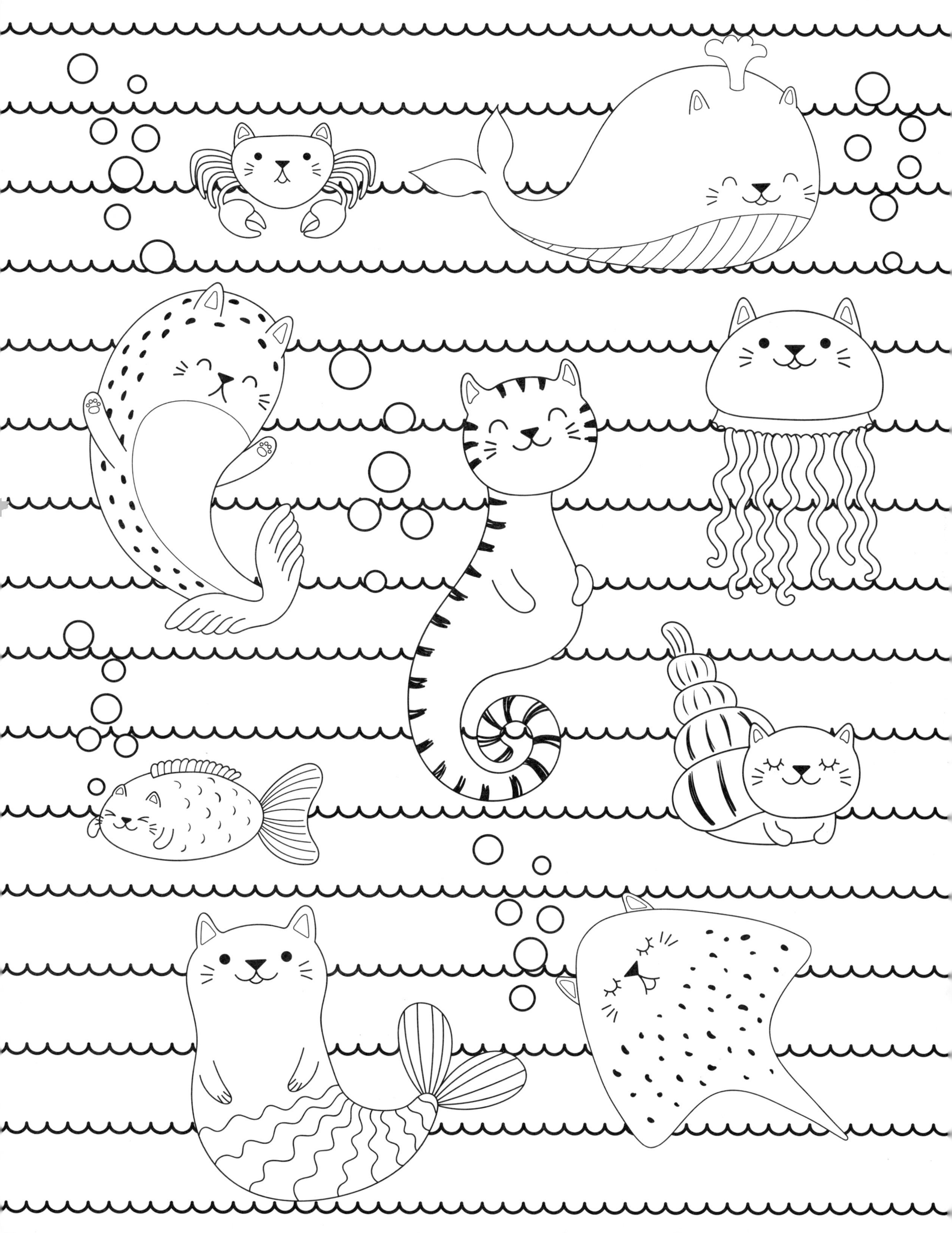

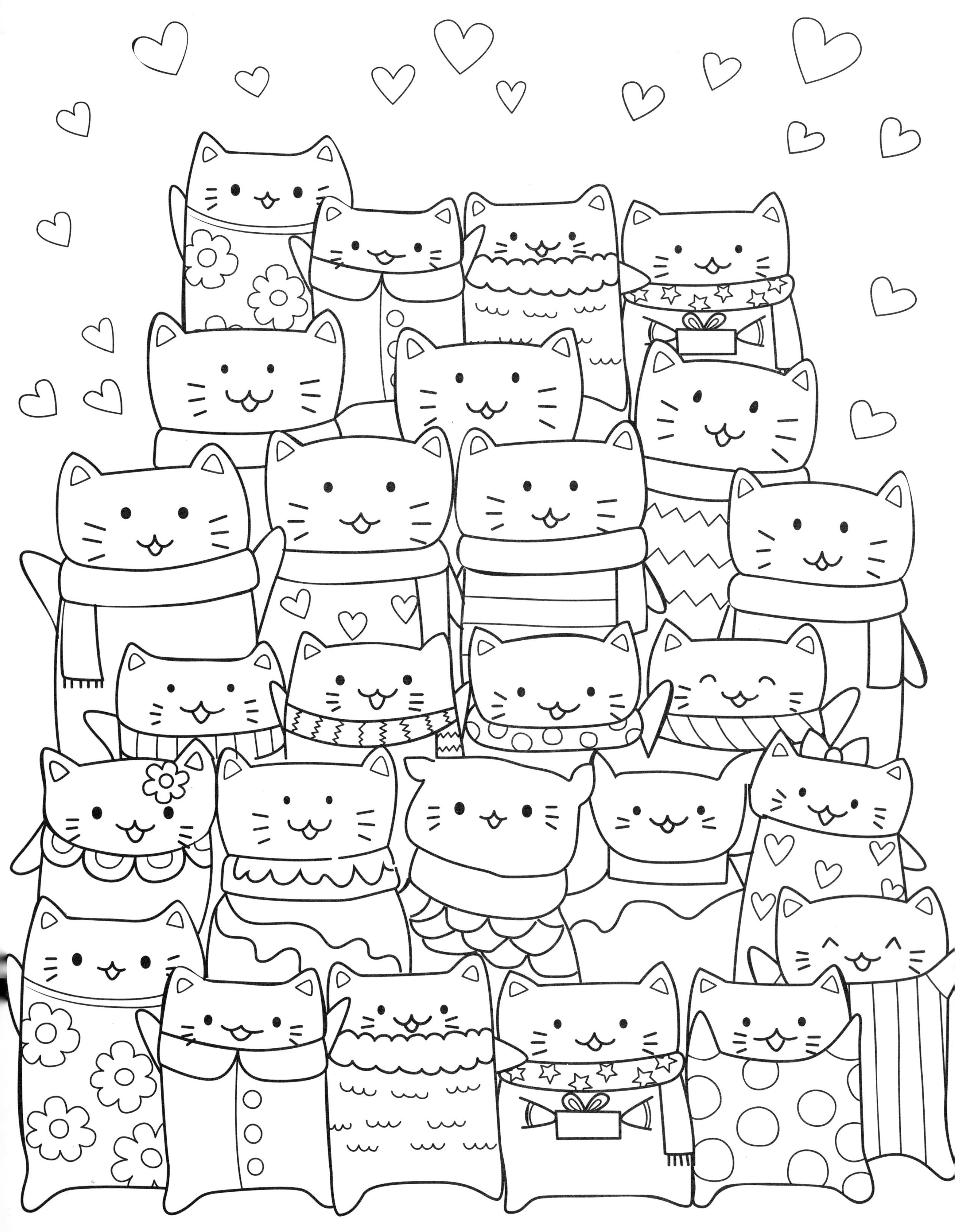

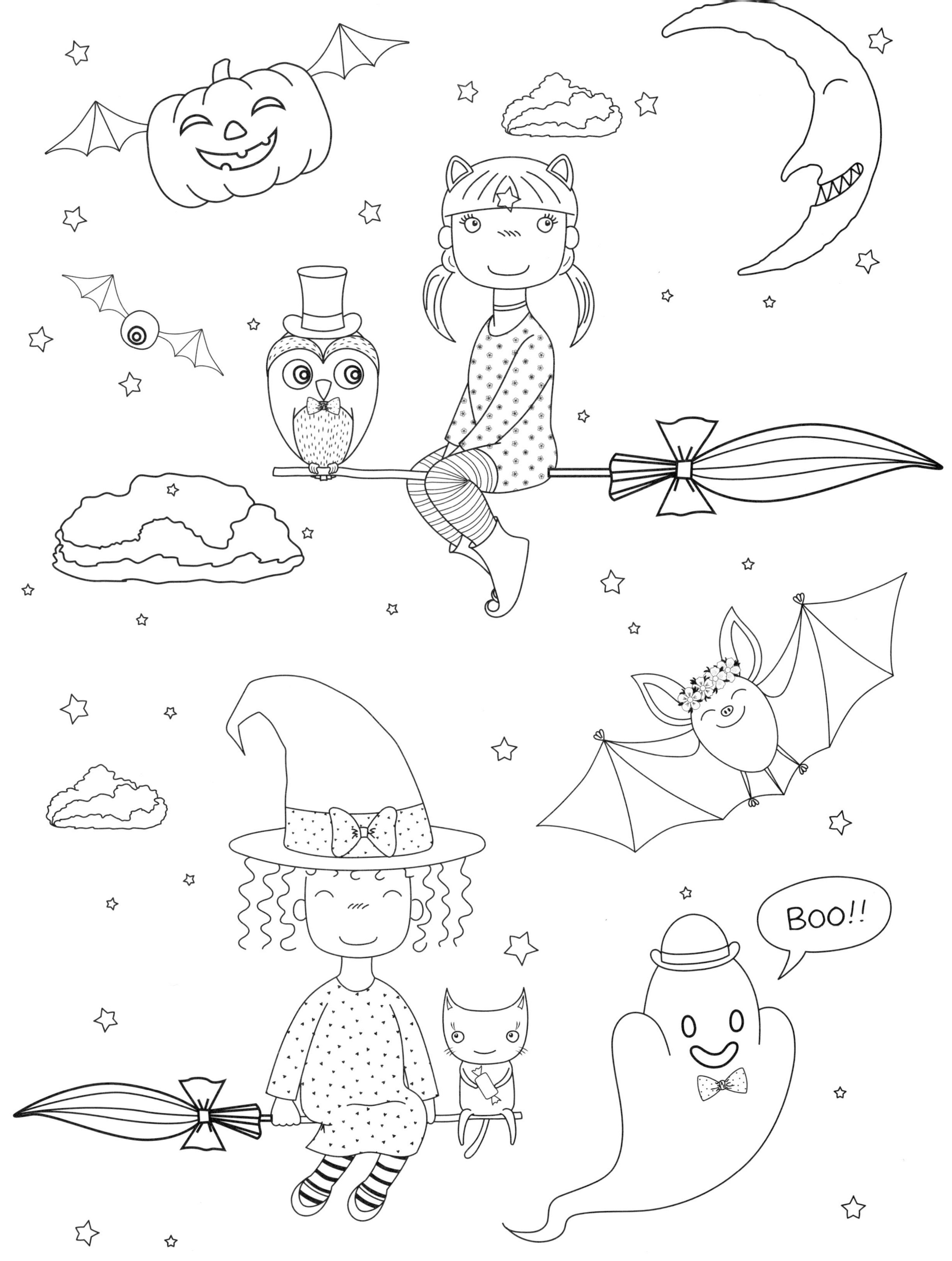
BOO!!

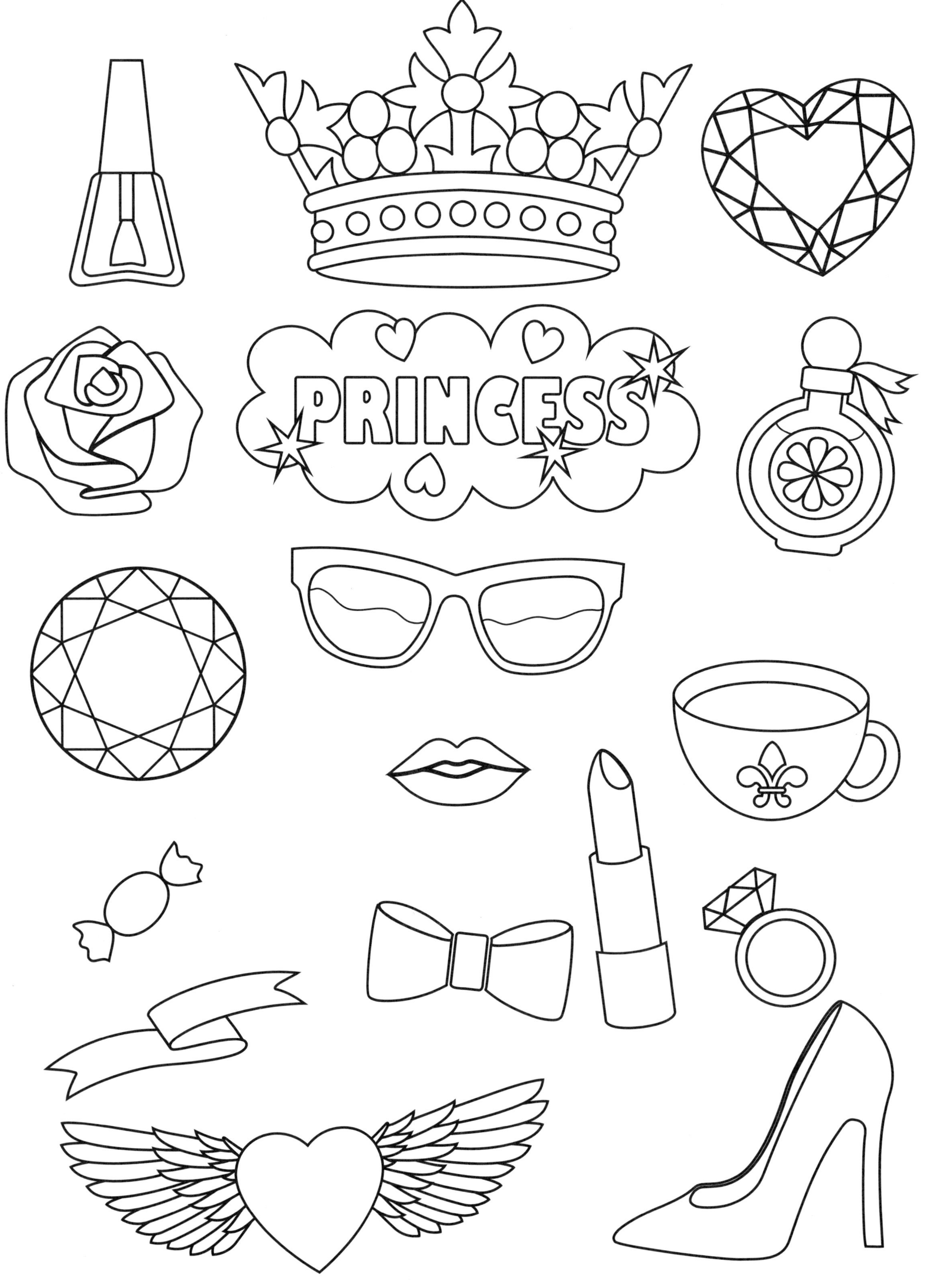
PRINCESS

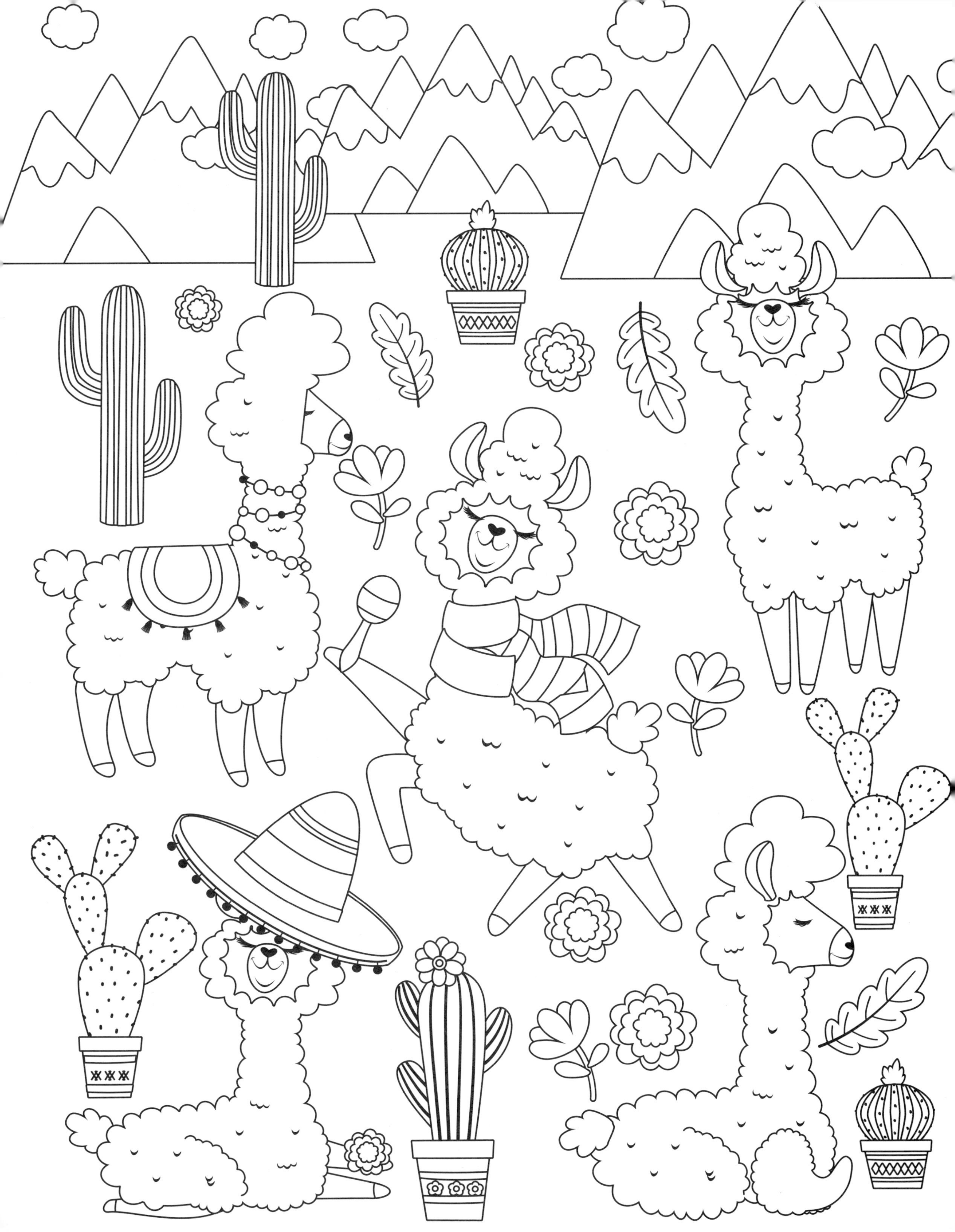

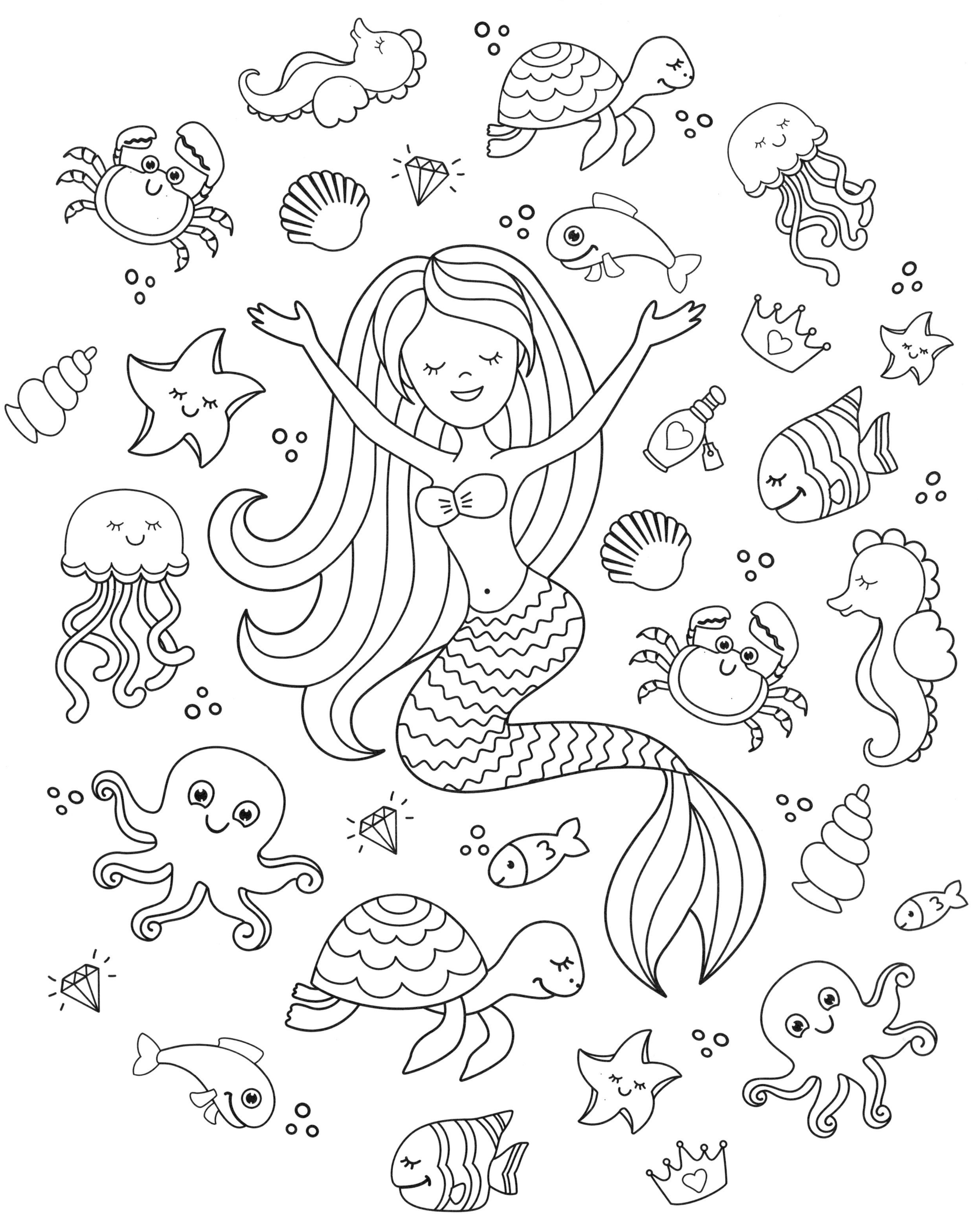

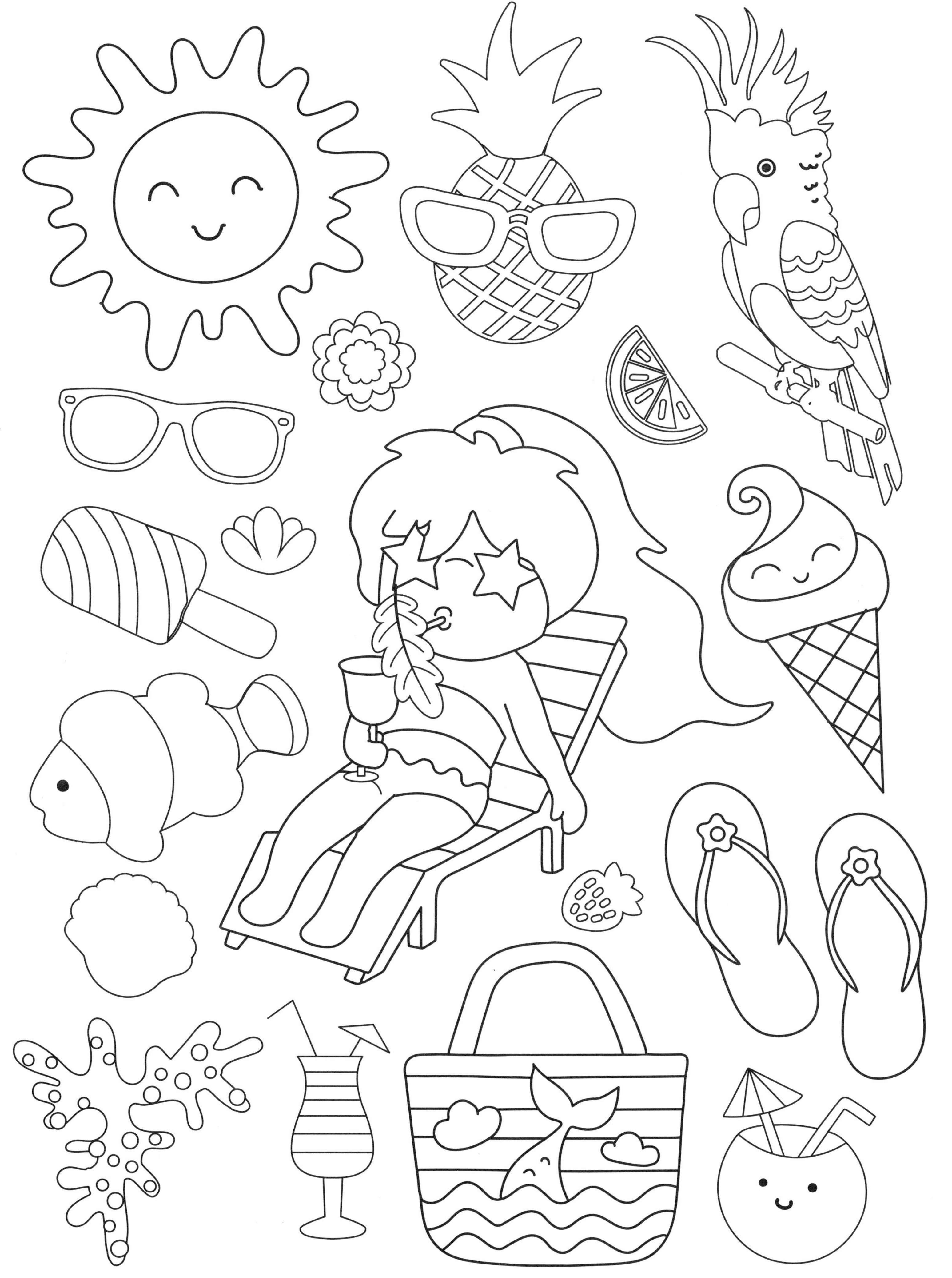

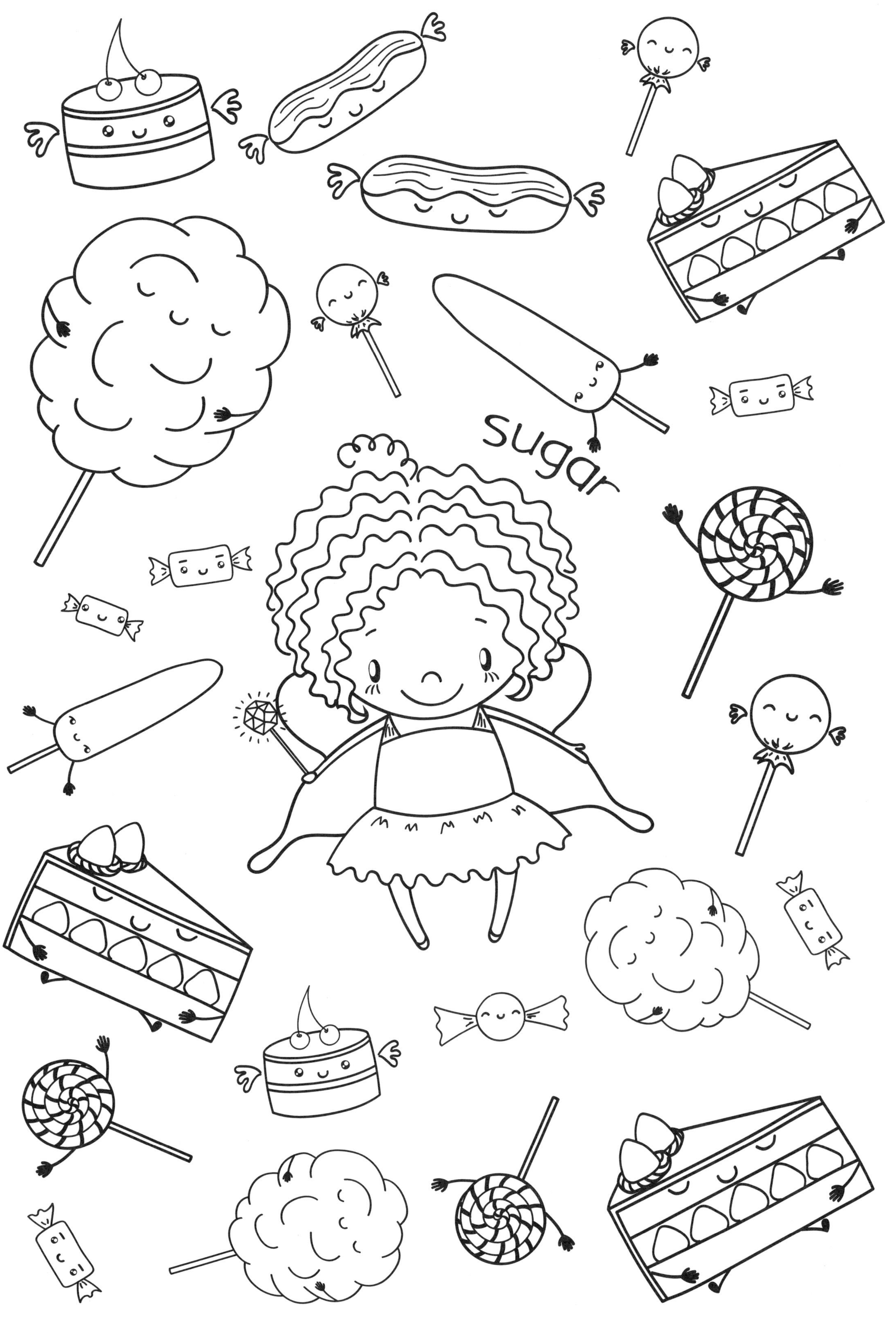
sugar

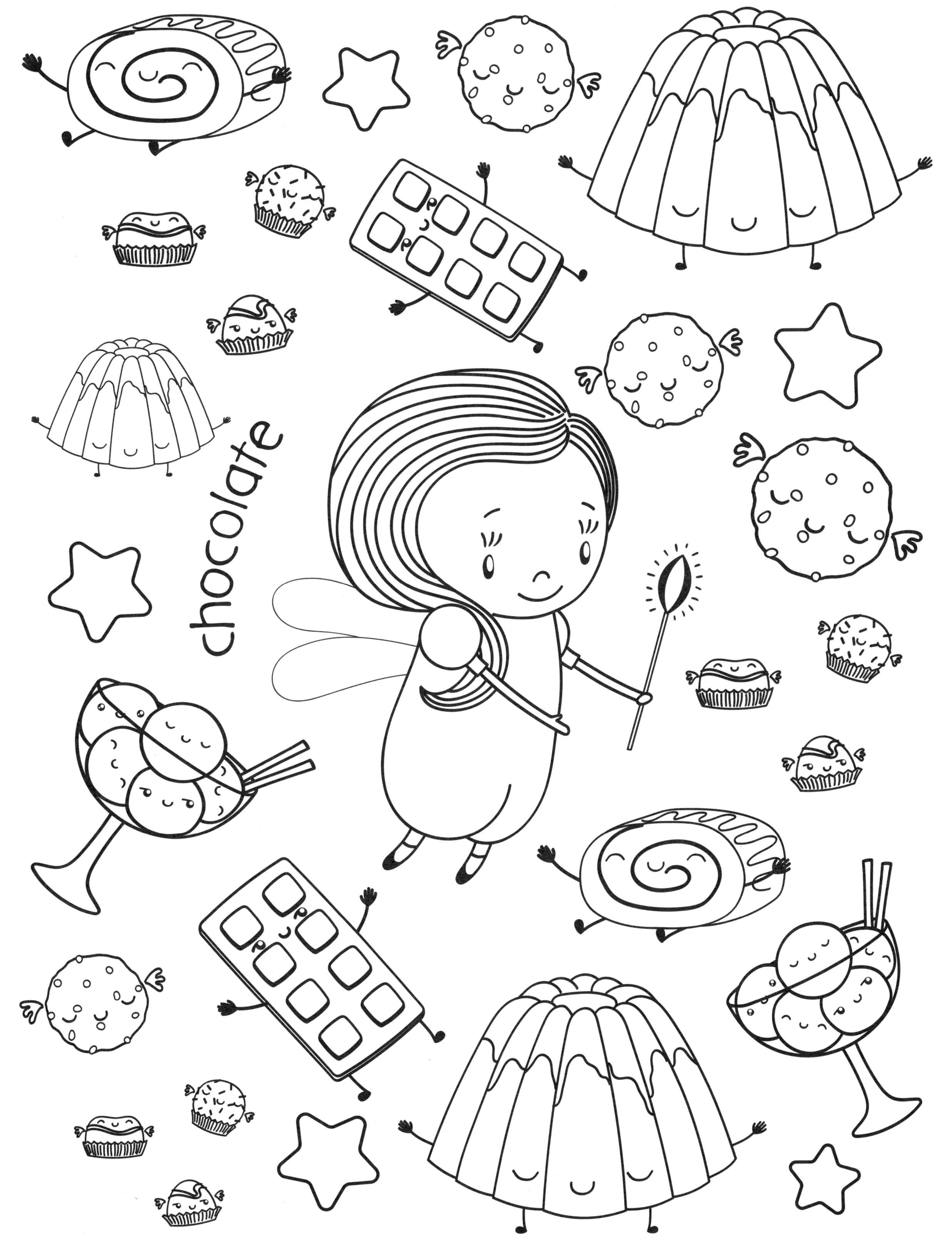
chocolate

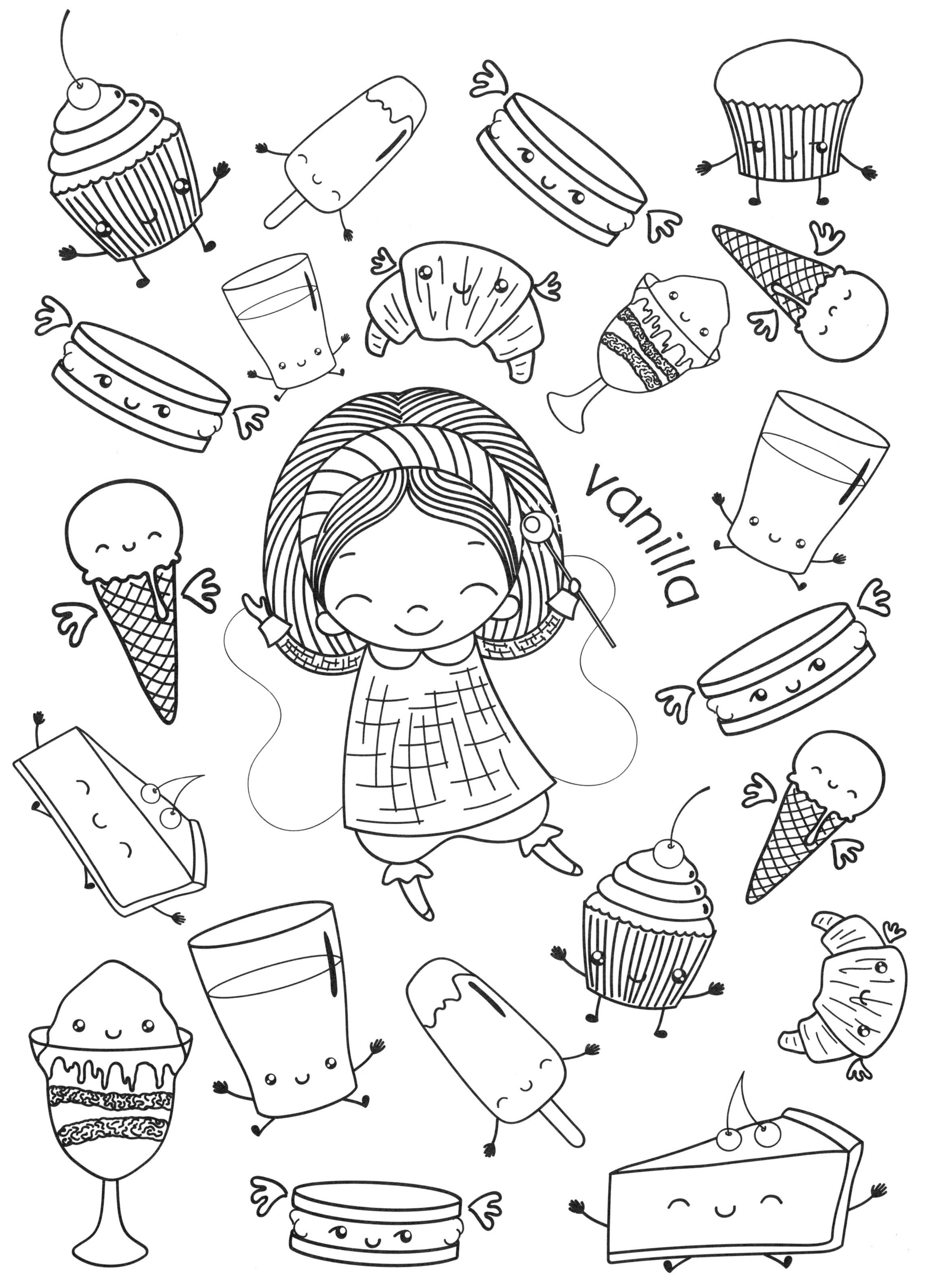
vanilla

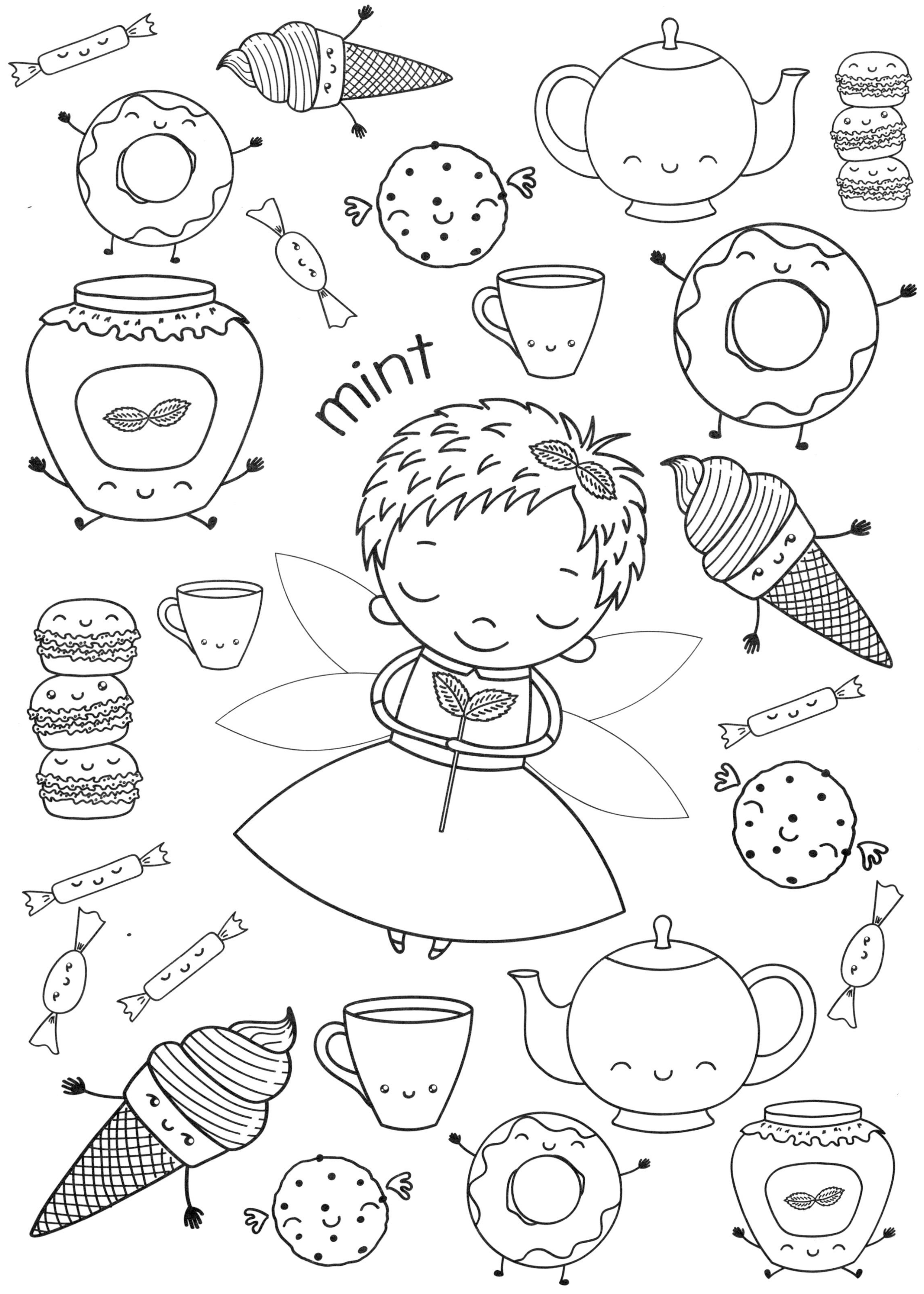
mint

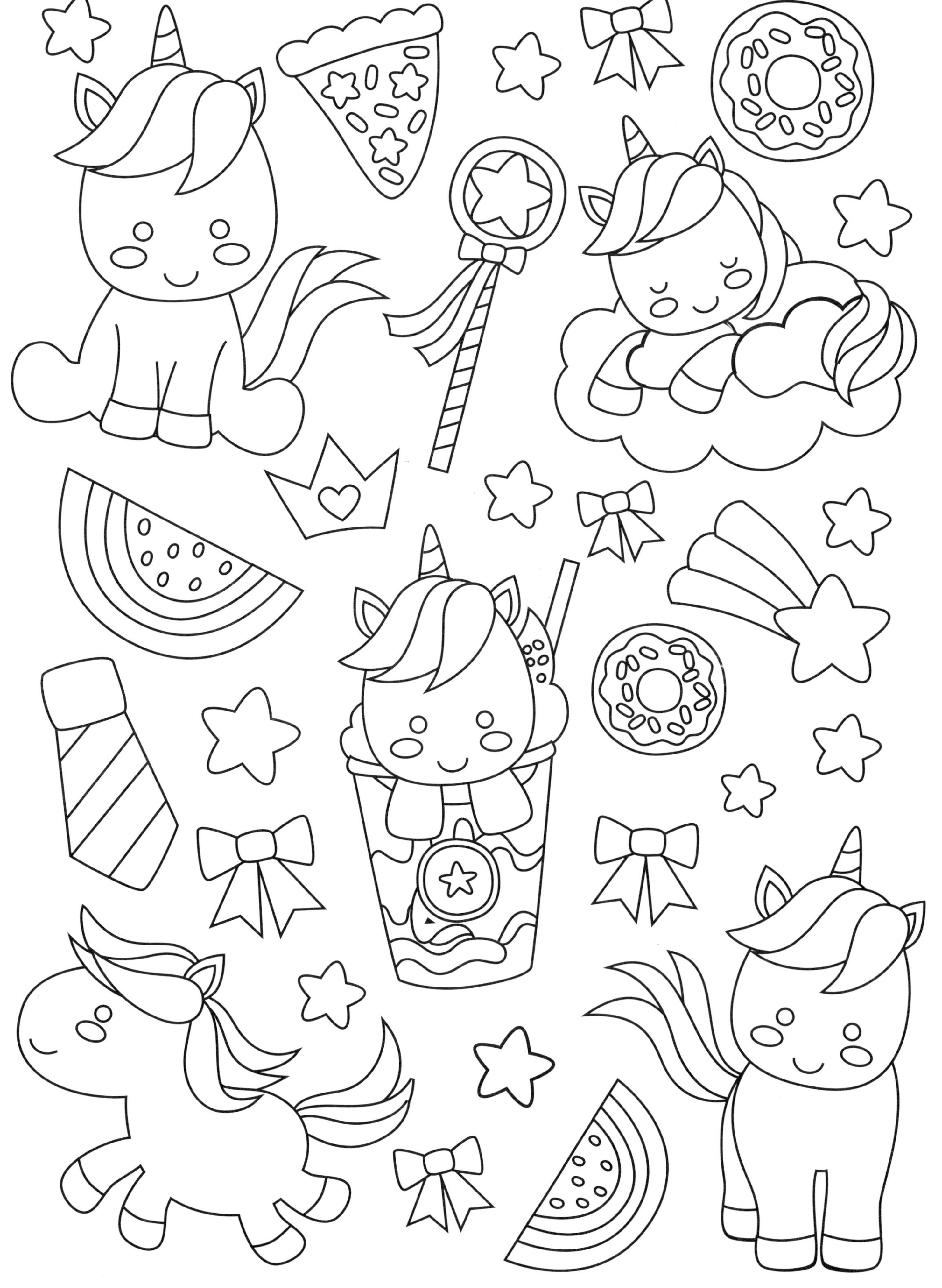

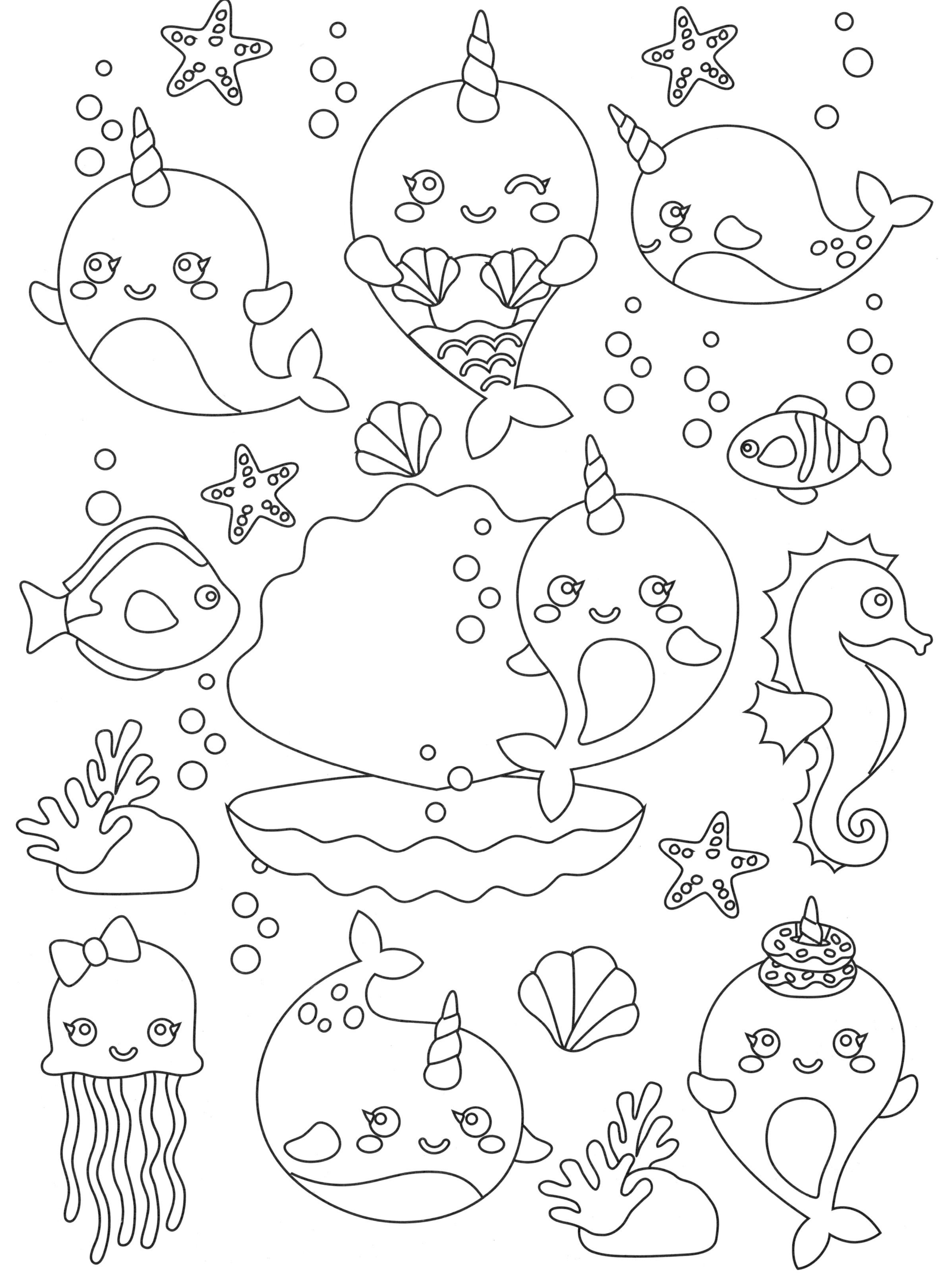

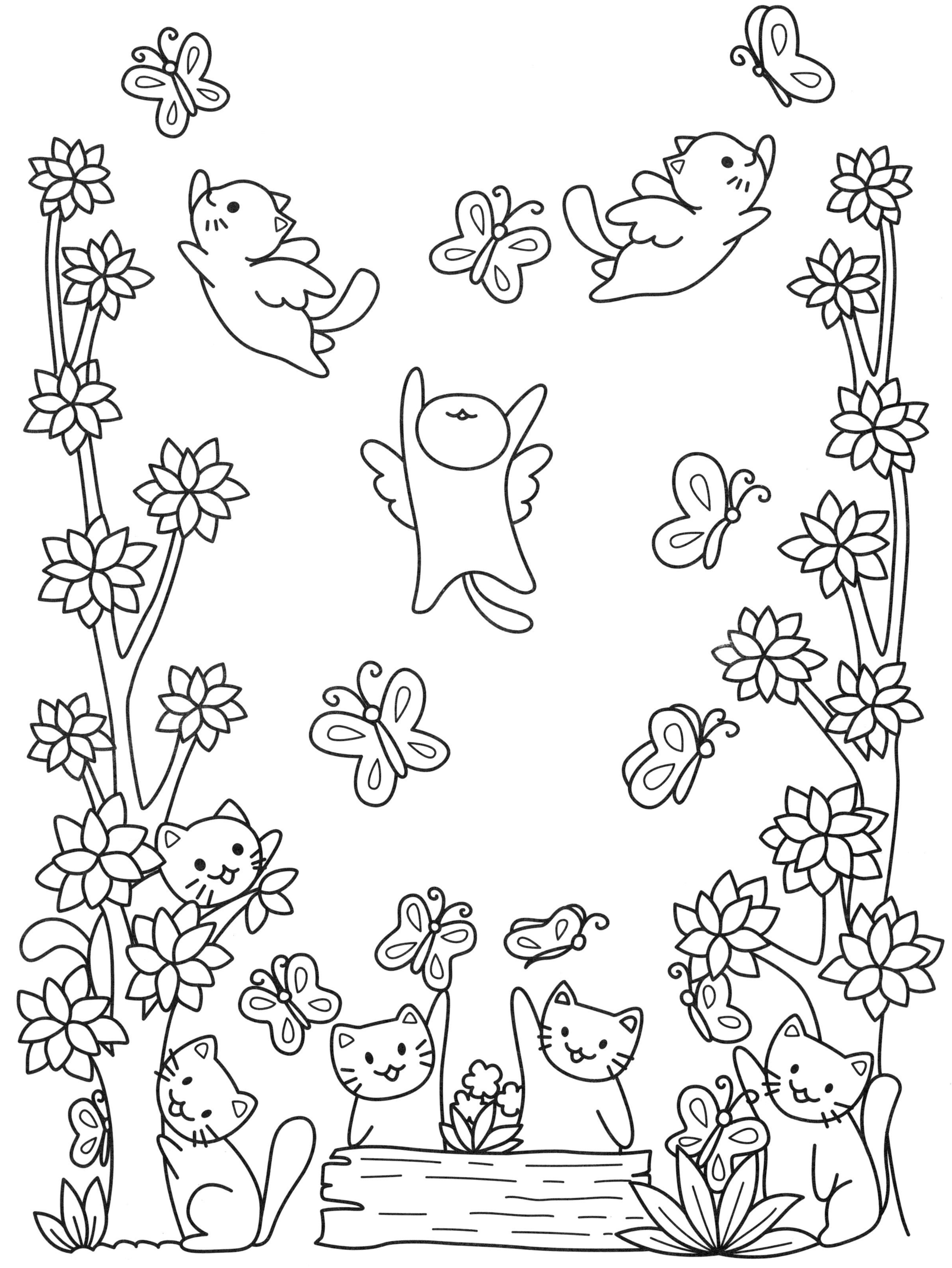

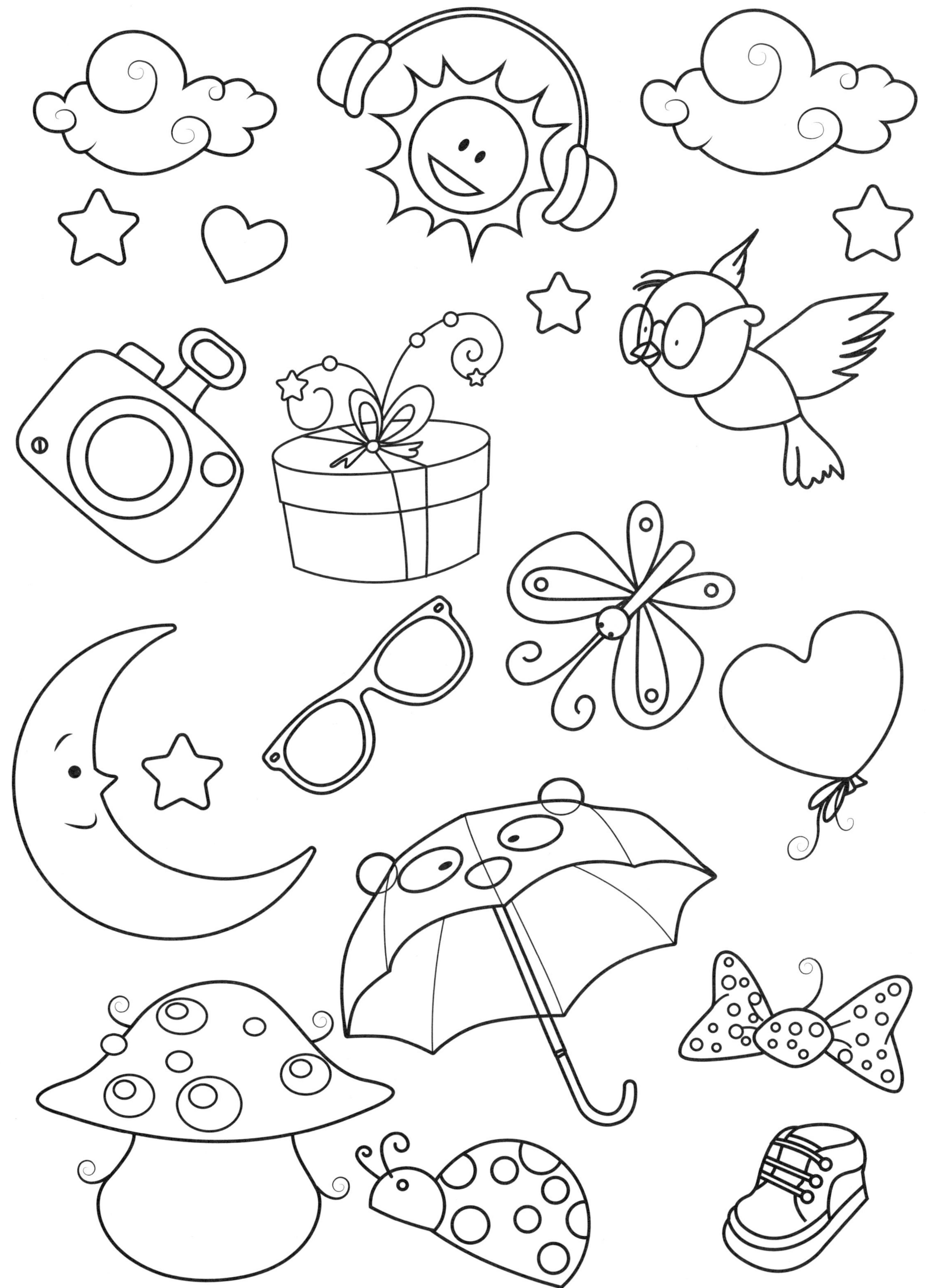

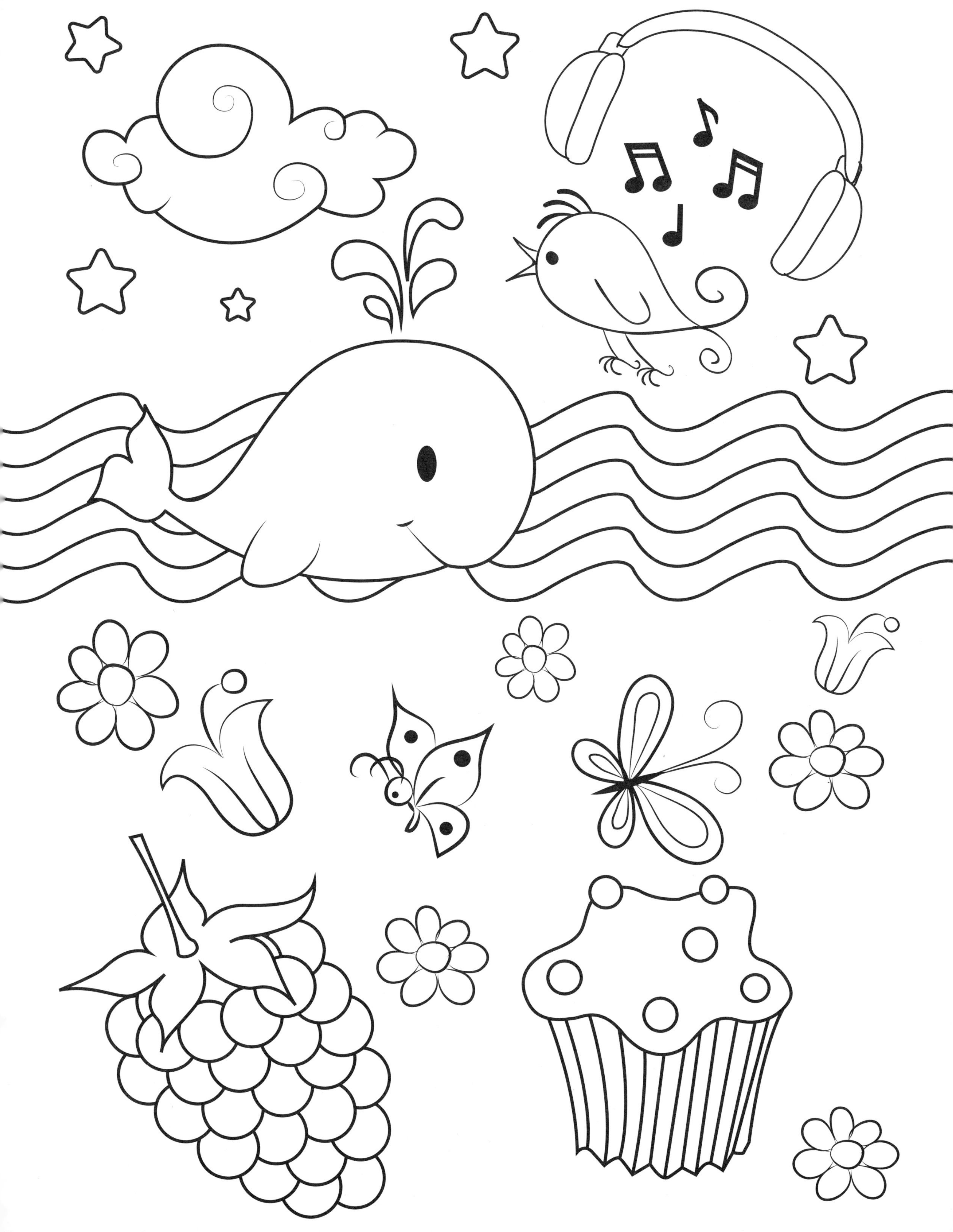

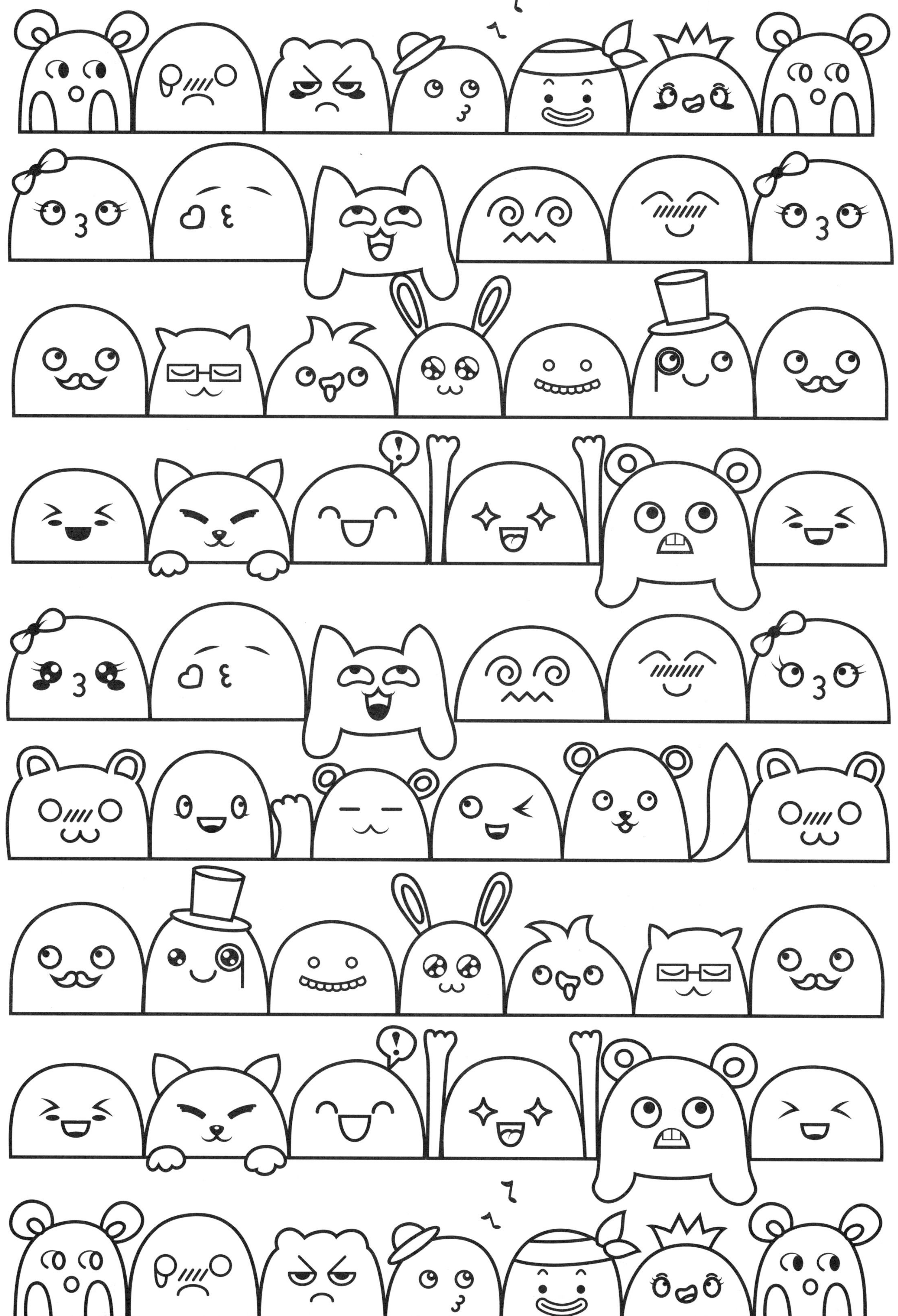

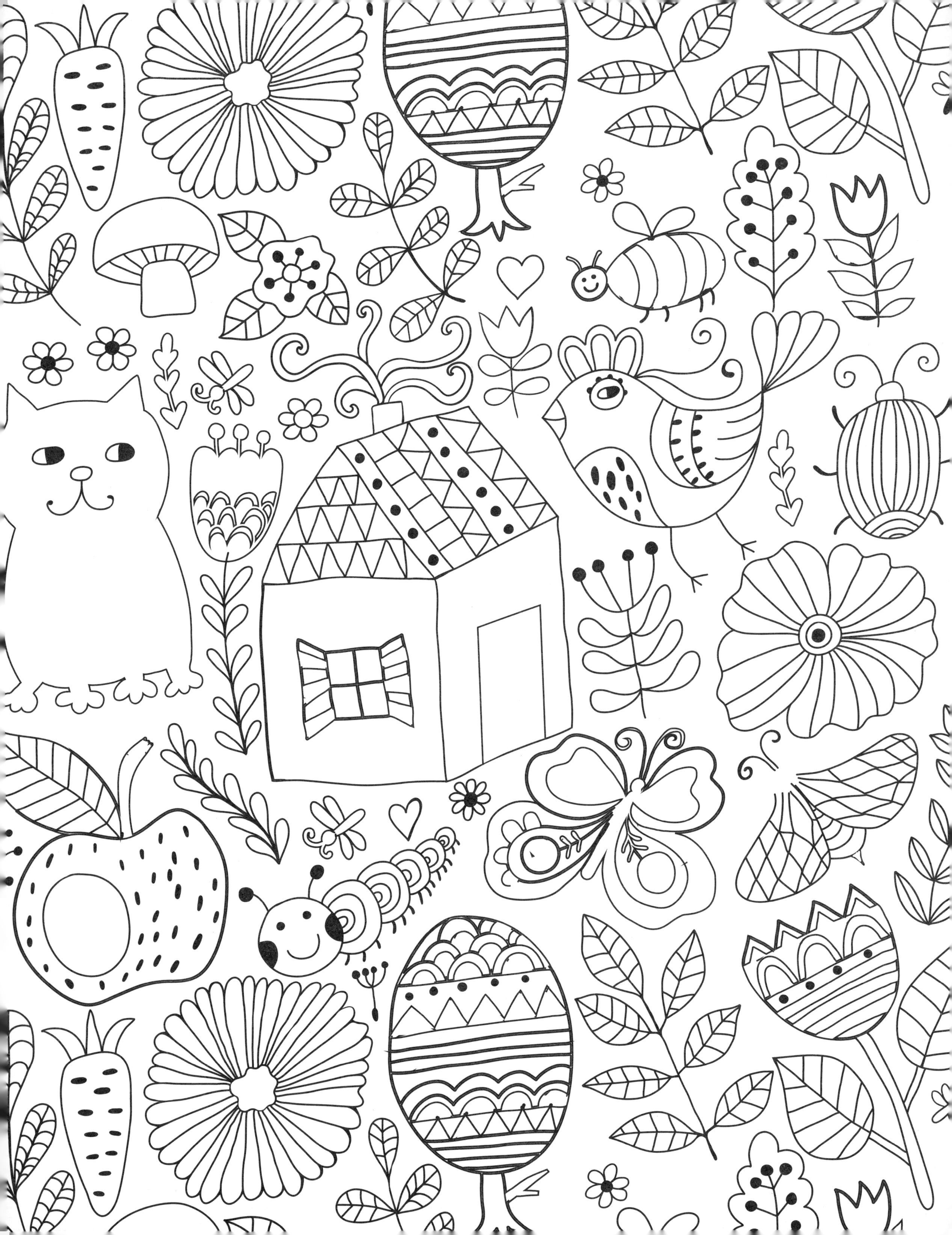

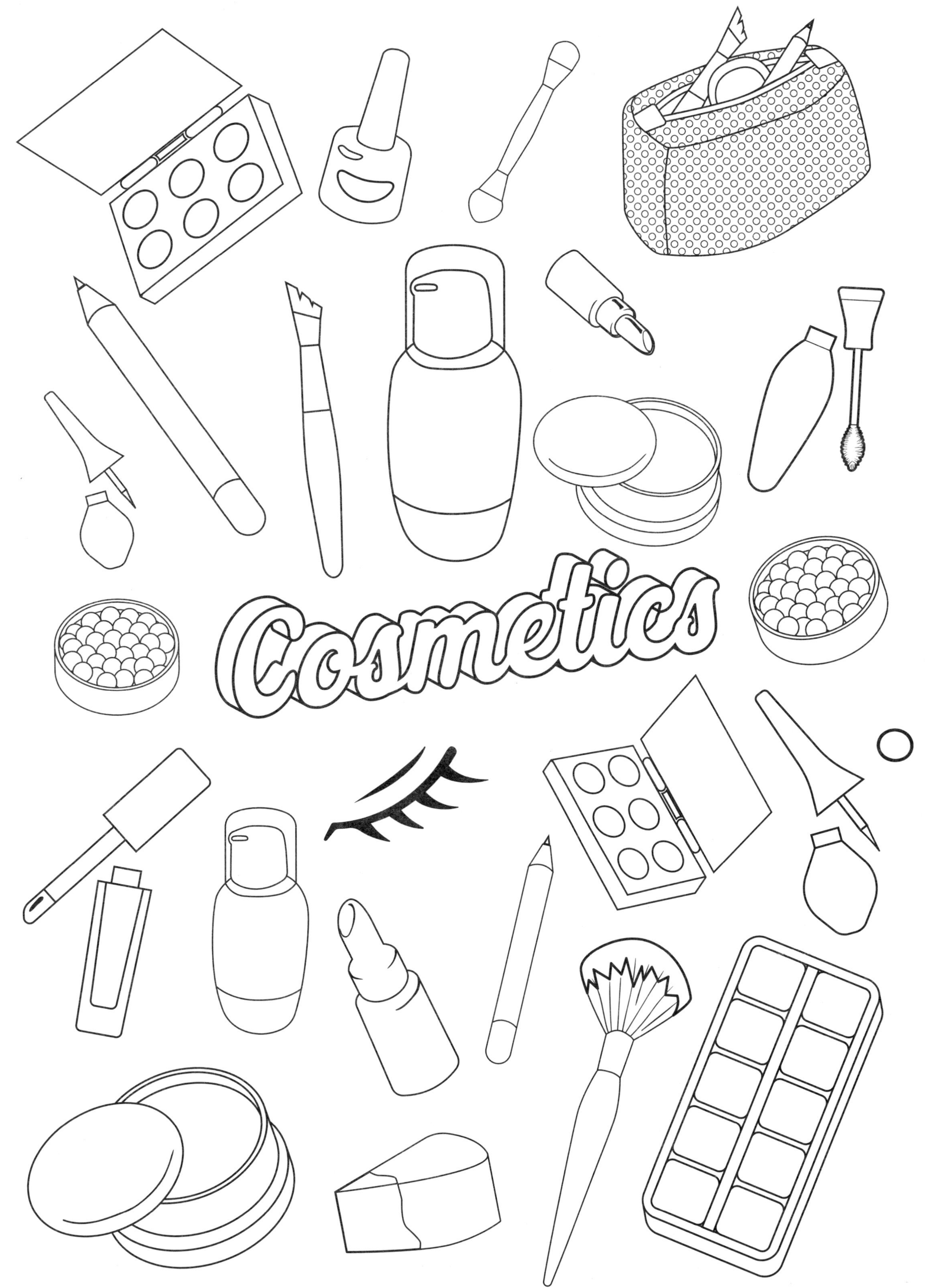
Cosmetics

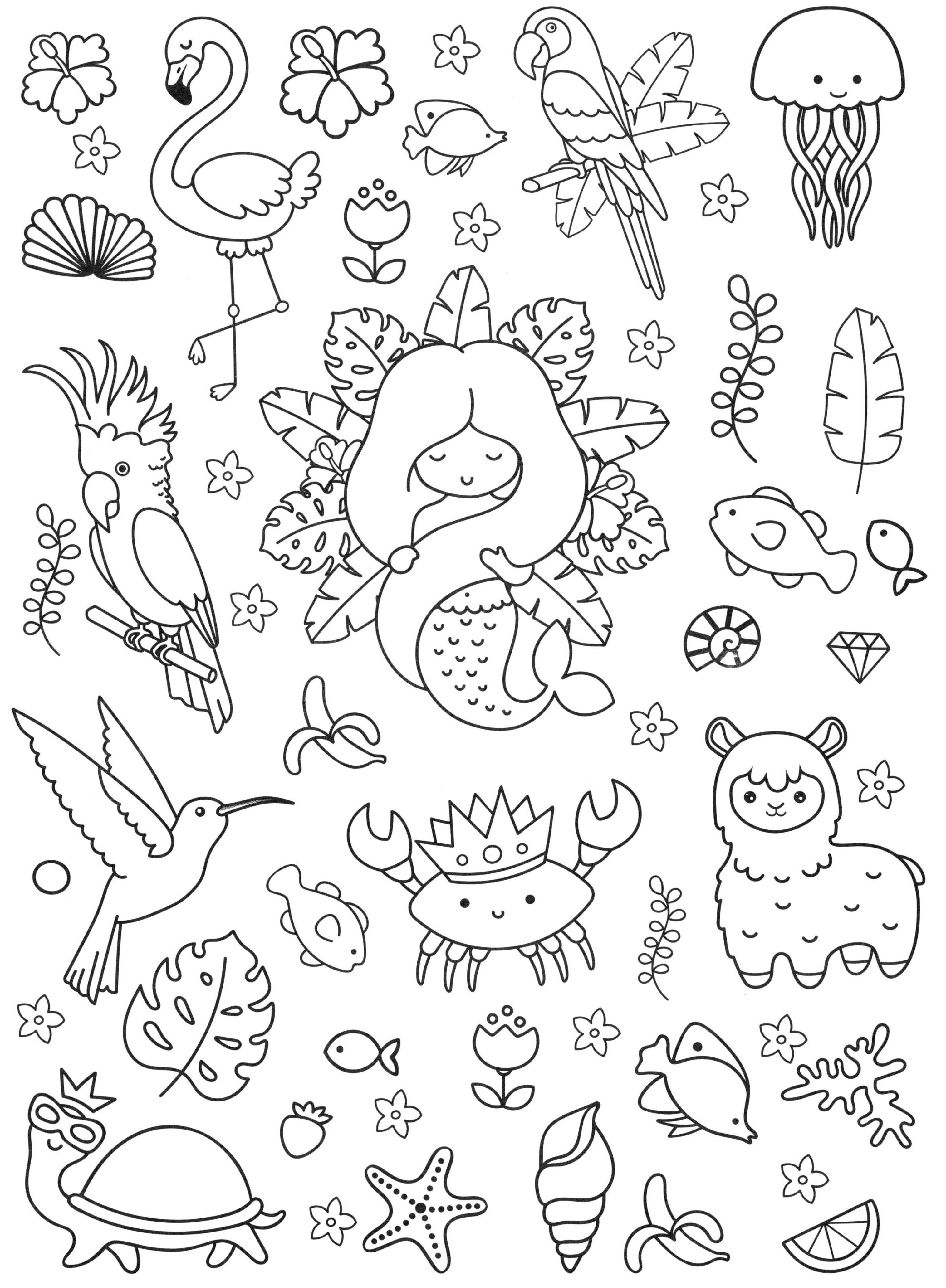

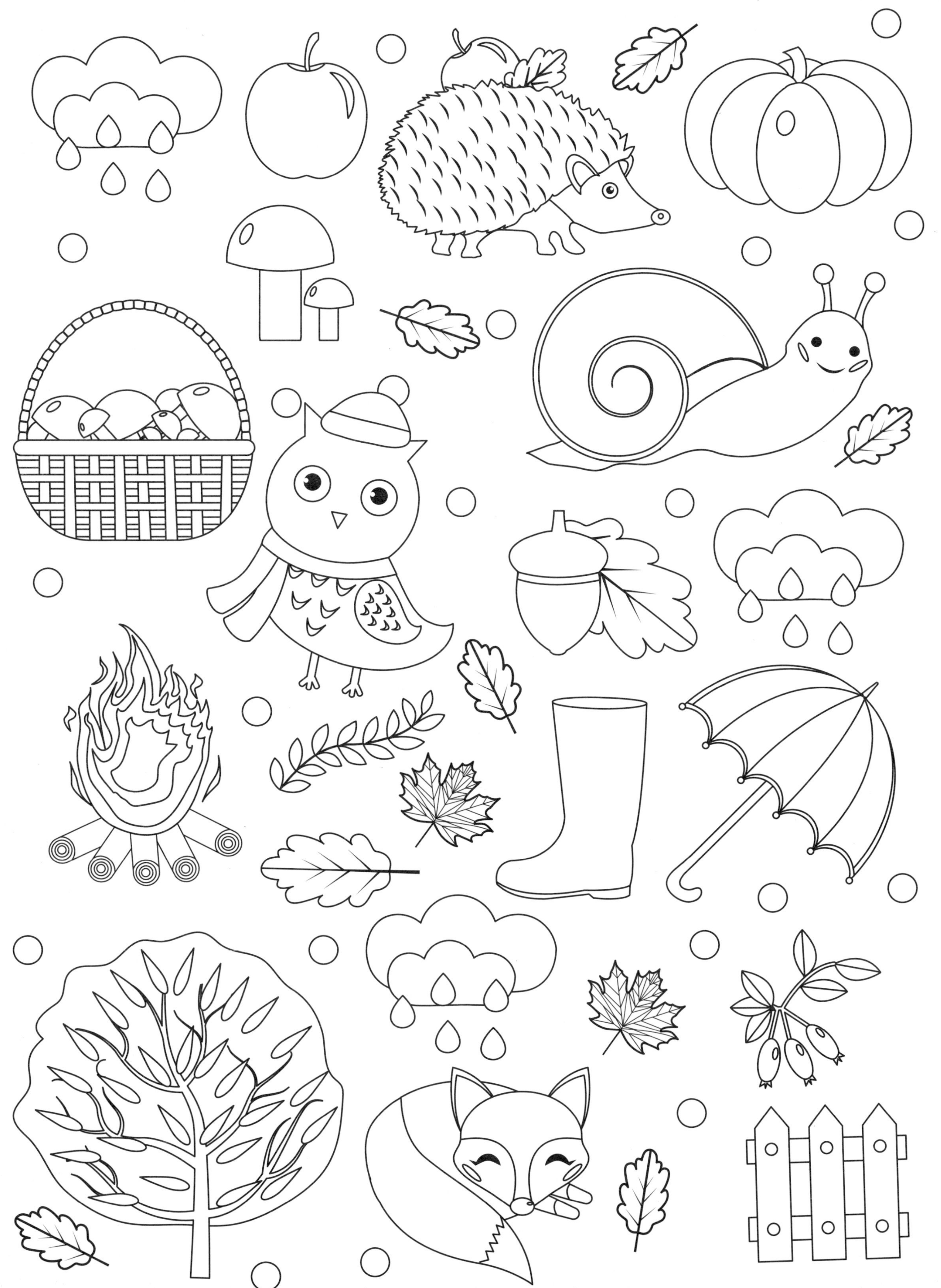

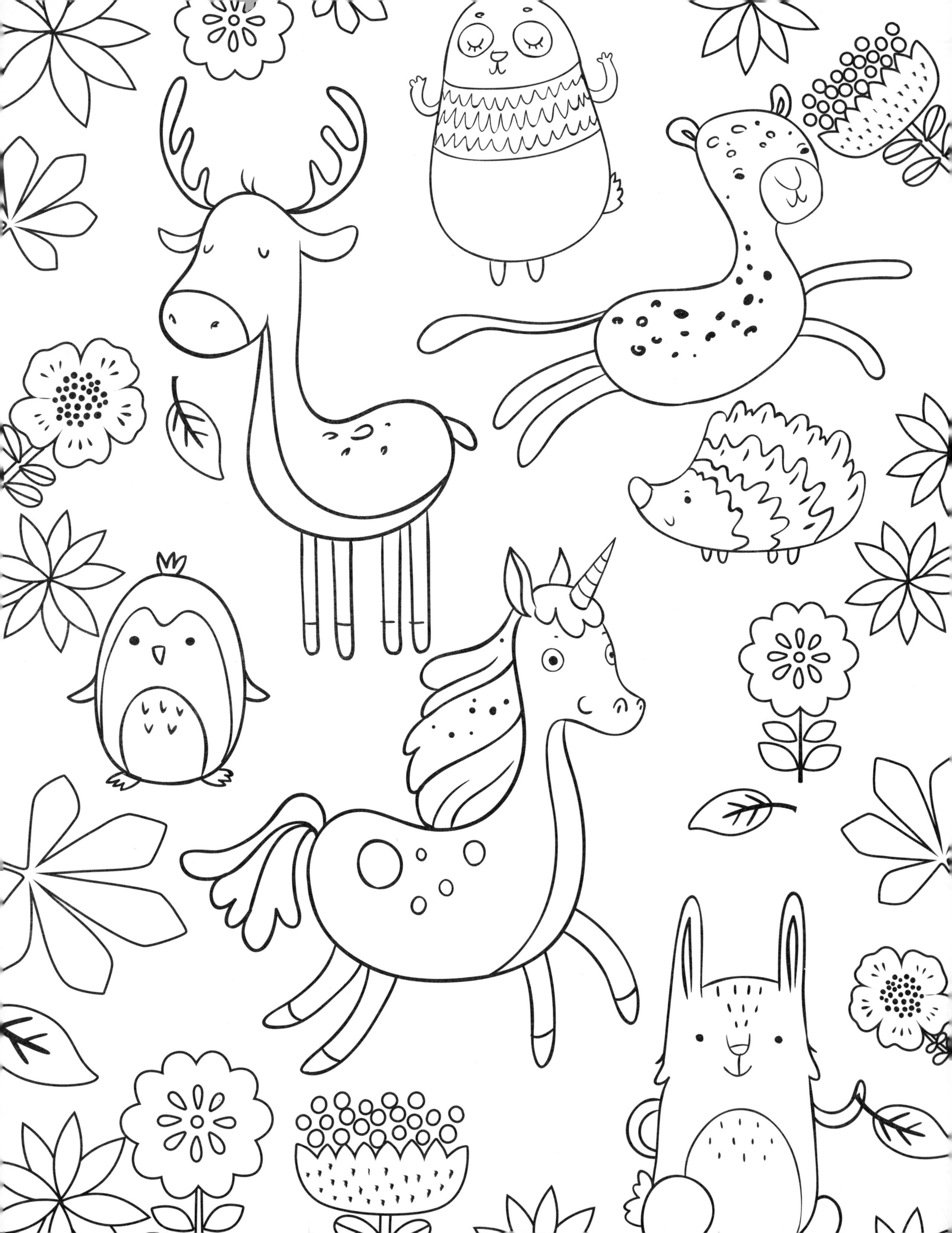